THE MAKING OF A LEADER

STEPPING STONES TO GREATNESS

ERICK SHOGHOLO

THE MAKING OF A LEADER
Stepping Stones to Greatness

Copyright © Erick Shogholo, 2020

Published by Erick Shogholo, Edmonton, Canada

ISBN 0-978-1-77354-214-0

*Dedicated to my beloved parents who
trained me to be who I'm today.*

Contents

PREFACE

True success in any line of work is not the result of chance or accident or destiny. It is the outworking of God's providence, the reward of faith and discretion, of virtue and perseverance. Fine mental qualities and high moral tone are not the result of accident. God gives opportunities; success depends upon the use made of them.[1]

Who is a leader in the making? A leader-in-making is a person who is pursuing understanding and applying the principles of leadership that have been used by successful leaders. Also, he or she gains insights from unsuccessful leaders, who disobeyed the natural laws of leadership and paid the penalty. The divine insight that they gain from the lives of these great leaders guide them to create, organize, plan, design and implement strategies that improve their life and the lives of their followers.

This wisdom helps them to connect with divine power to clearly see the future and inspire their followers to take actions that lead to that grand vision. At the same time, every action improves and inspires the team members to keep committing to the course, without deteriorating to segments of diverse ideologies.

The courage gained from people of faith motivates the leader to reassure their followers to keep pressing forward, though sometimes, the journey may get tough, when everything seems to be falling apart.

For more than 14 years, I have been moved by the desire to learn what makes great leaders influential and persuasive in inspiring people to create and reinvent their lives to a higher purpose in living. This inner longing propelled me to study the lives of great leaders—in politics, in science, in military, in religion, in business and in common walks of life.

I expanded my studies by learning the qualities of great leaders in the Bible: Adam, Noah, Abraham, Isaac, Jacob, Moses, Joshua, King David, King Solomon, Jesus, Peter and Paul. Their testimonies are full of life, purpose, faith and hard work.

I discovered one of the common attributes of these great leaders was that they were moved by one specific purpose in their lives. Whether they got their purpose in life through divine revelation or conviction, they believed in it and pursued it with all their might, committing every effort necessary to achieve it. For example, Abraham believed that, through his offspring, the world would be blessed. This compelling mission disciplined him to work harder to prepare for the success of his descendants.

Because of this compelling purpose, of becoming an influential leader and inspiring others to focus their energy and resources to become influential leaders as well, this book was born. You become a great leader by learning from wise men. Knowledge is progressive. You save time and precious resources by learning from those who propelled humanity's progress to date. Your time is very limited. To do the faithful work you were born to do, you're better off building on the work of those who laid the foundations. Even the great leader Jesus Christ built his work on the foundation of the prophets and patriarchs.

I searched for a model who has served as an influential leader in secular government, as well as served as a representative of the government of God. A leader who demonstrated the potential of what man could be when humanity's efforts unite with divine omnipotence in the spirit of harmony—that leader is Daniel.

Daniel proved to be very influential during his time; his biography and leadership legacy is recorded in the scroll of Daniel in the Old Testament. We will study his leadership skills and style to gain insight that will help us as leaders to improve our individual leadership abilities.

Daniel is the living testimony of courage, faith, integrity, wisdom, understanding, intelligence, hard work, knowledge, vision, foresight, humility and spiritual discernment. In addition to these, he was an educator, a communicator and a devoted master of leadership. The qualities a student of leadership would always look for when searching for a leadership mentor.

So, who was Daniel? He was a Jew forced into exile in Babylon around 605 BC, but through divine guidance, he became very influential and ascended Babylon's corridors of power and held powerful positions in the land; he became the governor of the province of Babylon during the kingship of Nebuchadnezzar. Also, King Nebuchadnezzar appointed Daniel as a chief of all the wise men and counselors in his palace.

He solved the hardest problems faced by the king, and through Daniel's guidance, the king governed his empire with great prosperity. Some complex problems that Daniel solved include interpretation of dreams (chapters 2 and 4 of the book of Daniel) and explaining writings scribed by the finger of God on a wall as a warning message to King Belshazzar.

During Darius's reign, he appointed Daniel as one of three administrators who oversaw the governance of the entire kingdom. Because his work ethic distinguished him from the rest of the leaders, the king honored him with a position of authority and power. Even the king planned to set Daniel above the entire kingdom, the testimony of the Living God who led and supported His servant.

He was a very devoted man of God, full of the Holy Spirit. The entire scroll of Daniel bears a testimony of the work of the Holy Spirit in the life of Daniel. Through the leading of the Holy Spirit, Daniel solved difficult problems, lived a holy life and honored his heavenly Father. Through the power of the Holy Spirit, he endured hardship with patience, understood the principles of the kingdom of Heaven and taught others to love and obey God. Not only that, he kept his connection with God through prayer.

His visions and prayers still influence the world and the Church after more than 2,600 years. Consider Daniel chapter 9: Daniel poured his heart out to God, seeking understanding and forgiveness for his people. Throughout these hours of soul searching, the Lord sent the angel Gabriel to give insight to Daniel concerning the future events for God's people: the restoration of Jerusalem and her glory, and the revealing of the Messiah for all humankind.

His legacy, as recorded in the book of Daniel, is full of prophecy: dreams and visions bearing the records of the rise and fall of nations since the inception of the kingdom of Babylon and her fall; He prophesied concerning the rise of the Median, Persian and Greek empires and their falls, as well as the formation of the Roman empire and the rise of the religious Roman kingdom.

His prophecy helps God's people continue to persevere and hope amidst persecution and difficult times. His prophecy proves that God is still in control of this world. No matter how the world is corrupted, the Sovereign God is still steering this world toward his divine purpose.

How did Daniel become such a powerful leader?

Before Daniel became an influential leader in a foreign country and to the world, the Lord placed him in a school of leadership in Babylon to be trained, so he could develop his abilities to the level of a masterful leader. Also, Daniel learned from those leaders who committed themselves to the cause of righteousness: the prophet Jeremiah, Moses, Isaiah, Ezekiel, Joshua, Abraham, Isaac and Jacob—the very process that we will take to learn and gain insight and discernment.

In this book, I have analyzed the broad leadership principles that Daniel established as a leader while serving under King Nebuchadnezzar, Darius, Cyrus and Belshazzar.

These precious leadership principles include: the importance of training; hardship as the source of renewal; establishing a solid values system; the power of prayer in the leader's life; the influence of mutual friends; God's favor; the influence of the Holy Spirit; seeking understanding; the value of service to others; the qualities that make the student of leadership successful; skills in solving difficult problems; dealing with your superiors; the art of communication; developing an inspiring vision and mission; and planning and working for your legacy.

These gold-like principles equipped Daniel and supplied a solid foundation for his leadership. He recorded them in his writings, so we may gain wisdom and insight in developing our potential to the highest standards possible.

I distilled these principles from his writings, then expanded them with a broader view of understanding of the biblical leadership principles, relating them with other great leaders from the Bible. In addition to these applications, I widen my understanding of these principles by bringing commentaries and ideas of great leaders like Abraham Lincoln, John F. Kennedy, Baraka Obama, Nelson Mandela, Mahatma Gandhi, Isaac Newton, Thomas Edison, Albert Einstein, Alexander the Great, Ellen G. White, John Maxwell, Stephen Covey and Tony Robbins. The reason for bringing insight from various leaders is so we may be well-balanced and successful leaders. The principles of leadership behoove us to harmonize our spiritual leadership and our day-to-day work.

The best way to benefit from this book is to read it with an open mind, reflect on your leadership journey—where you have been successful and where you failed—and see if it was because you ignored one of these principles presented in this book. Put the principle to work and devise the best strategy on how you can apply it at work. Read the Bible with a leader's mindset, noting every key leadership lesson you gain from the Bible's characters and comparing the principle with other great leaders in business, politics, science and military to produce a deeper understanding of the principle.

You may visit and read the book of Daniel; it would be wise not to concern yourself too much with understanding the prophecy recorded in it—focus on what made Daniel such a powerful leader. Discuss with a few other leaders, see how they have applied these principles and find the best way to implement them in your own life.

CHAPTER 1

LEADERSHIP

What is leadership? Many of us have a misconception about leadership. When we speak about leadership, we jump to mention positions, like president, CEO, director, manager, husband or wife. We think this is leadership, and then we beat ourselves on the chest, "I cannot achieve that, it is too high for me." But these are positions.

Sadly, some prominent leaders want you to believe that they were born to be there; but you do not deserve to lead—this is the greatest lie of all. This is why I'm doing this project: to open your eyes, so you can see clearly. As one author said, "Whether you're a CEO, a self-employed professional, a stock room clerk, a receptionist, a stay-at-home parent, or a good friend, to someone—whatever you do, at times you are a leader. What you do every day—what people see you do—is a reflection on yourself."[2] Sharing the beautiful character inside of you with the world—that is leadership.

Leadership is not a position; rather, it is an influence. Leadership is the ability to influence people to follow your vision or to help them discover their purpose in life and follow it through. Then, a leadership position is a tool given to a leader to exercise authority and power. Position gives a mandate to a leader to exercise power. Position is just like a sword—if the leader doesn't know how to wield it skillfully, the position will destroy the leader and the followers. But if they are a competent leader, a position will prove to be a blessing.

There are wise leaders and foolish leaders; it all depends on the training and condition of the heart of the leader. So, leadership boils down to personal leadership and management; the moment you master leading yourself wisely to achieve your goals and manage and control your own heart, seek to bless others with a spirit of humility—that is leadership. You do not have to hold a powerful position to be an influential leader.

Jesus did not have a formal position in the counsel of Sanhedrin, but he changed the world. Mahatma Gandhi did not hold a powerful position as a politician in the British government, but he led the nation of India to independence.

I hold this truth about the most powerful leaders in the world: their glory is not spoken often, or we do not appreciate their works as we should; our parents, especially our mothers. To be a husband/father or wife/mother is a position that comes with the responsibilities of the marriage covenant, but to be a wise and understanding husband or wife requires leadership skills.

Leaders are influential because of who they are inside, because they have a compelling vision and have the perseverance to achieve that vision which they have designed for themselves or with their followers. As one influential leader wrote in his book *Servant Leadership*: "Leadership is about going somewhere; it's not wandering aimlessly."[3] Leaders create companies, organizations, kingdoms and empires. When you study the history of great empires, most of them were organized by one leader with an inspiring vision, who knew how to mobilize people in a common purpose and follow it through.

Some leaders prove to be wise, understanding and helpful, so people bestow them with a position of authority so they can exert more influence on society and change it for better.

Let me correct one myth held by many people: to become a powerful leader, you must be born in a certain cast of people in a society. I believe that if you identify your gifts and develop them, you will be an influential leader in your area of service. Some individuals are born to fulfill a specific position in the society, but that does not make them successful leaders; they still must go through training and prove themselves to be wise and visionary individuals.

WHO IS A LEADER, AND WHAT ARE THE ROLES OF A LEADER?

To understand who a leader is, in depth, let us consider a human brain. The brain is one of the fascinating and complex organs in the human body. In simple terms, the brain is protected in a shell called the skull, above the neck. Inside that skull is a round-like shape of tissue composed of water, blood vessels and interconnected nerves.

As much as science and technology have increased, scientists have not fully comprehended the depth and the mystery of this organ. Though, through scanning, they have been able to map the brain and understand how various parts of the brain relate to the whole system of the human body.

Without the brain, the living body is just a figure. This makes the human brain vital for normal functioning and the well-being of our body and those around us. The human brain is at the center of every activity that occurs internally and externally of a human body.

The brain functions as a receiver and processor of information, a coordinator of all activities that happen inside the human body, a network hub, a director of actions, a resources manager, a store of information, a vision formulator, a decision maker, a center of consciousness. Many functions are performed under the watchfulness and coordination of the brain. If today, you were to lose your brain, you would lose your sense of purpose and direction.

As the brain functions as the pillar for the human's well-being and prosperity, so does a leader. A leader is the brain of a family, an organization, a church, a cooperation or a country. The leader is the heart of organizing and running an enterprise to function effectively and succeed in its mission. If there is no leader, the whole body is useless: food for scavengers. If the brain functions at capacity; the human organisms succeed and excel—life is joyful and peaceful—but if the brain is not normal, the entire body suffers. Beautiful brains are the springs of great actions that transforms people and society.

We all have met with individuals like this, which may be painful and saddening. They have lost their sense of purpose, and as a result, their lives are miserable and disheartening. For some, no matter how you try to help them, they are pulled back to their difficulties.

That is what happens when there is a lack of effective leadership in any organization or at a personal level; if a person cannot lead themselves well, their life is a shamble. Lack of leadership creates disunity, disharmony, confusion, laziness and at the highest level of this foolishness, the people perish. As King Solomon once said, "where there is no vision, the people perish."[4] Where there is no leader, people perish. As a healthy brain is vital to the well-being of an individual, so is effective leadership vital for the prosperity of society.

There is no perfect leader, as there is no perfect brain—we are all striving to achieve that perfection. We should understand that the level of leadership differs from one individual to another. Some leaders are well-trained and well-disciplined in inspiring others to achieve wonders, others are still growing and learning. I believe each one of us are at some level of development. Until death do us part, no one will reach the limit of learning to become a great leader. What does this mean? We are all students, and some are experienced compare to others. So, we must keep learning to be better; it should be a goal for each one of us, to keep learning.

A human brain is a learning machine. It learns anything that passes across it; there is no limit for brain development in terms of knowledge and capacity. You can stretch that organ as far as you can, but you can never stop it from learning. As a leader, you keep learning innovative ideas that will make you valuable.

The roles of a leader are like that of the brain. As a leader, it is vital to know and acquaint yourself with varied functions or roles of a leader. Knowing what your roles are, in any project, will give you clarity of thought and motivation to work hard to achieve those objectives you planned as a team.

A LEADER IS A RESOURCE MANAGER

The brain manages the resources available in the body, allocating them to ensure the well-being of the human body. The brain has an active role in doing this job. For example, if your muscles need calories for you to keep running, your muscles will use what is available at the moment and inform the brain to command other organs of the body that have extra to share the needed energy. If the brain perceives that you need more calories, then it will go through its process, and you will run to the store to pick up a fruit, eat it, digest it and send calories where they are needed the most to sustain you. If there is no food around to sustain you, your body, in coordination with brain, will try to share resources until such time as food will be available. If nothing happens, then the system will collapse.

The leader functions as a steward of the organization's resources. It is the work of a leader to know where resources are, where to find more and where to move them to produce the greatest return. Many times, the leader functions in an environment where resources are scarce, and it is his responsibility to ensure they put those available resources to a beneficial use. If there is a need, he or she makes sure to collaborate with his team to increase what is lacking to ensure the system works efficiently.

The leader must be well-trained to manage resources, such as money, talents and equipment. The tools that will make his work productive must be installed. The leader must make sure they unite with those faithful individuals who are well-trained to better use the resources to help the whole system.

A LEADER IS A DECISION MAKER

The main function of a brain is decision maker. When a person's ear detects a change of wavelength in a room, it will transmit that information from the ear, through the nervous system to the brain, and the brain decodes the message; as a result, it decides what kind of sound it is. If, according to its store data, the sound requires immediate action—either flee, fight or freeze—then the brain sends information to the hand: pick up the blanket and run to a master point for more information.

The main purpose of a brain's decision mechanism is to facilitate action. Without decision, there is no action.

The equivalent mechanism applies to a leader. When a leader receives information, he or she processes it according to the established system. Some decisions that the leader will encounter in his or her career include financial, investment, human capital management, production and development decisions.

Then, concurring to a decision requirement, he or she assigns skilled people to take those actions that will guarantee the success of that decision. If a decision requires an immediate response, they must be quick to act. If the leader is weak in deciding, they endanger everyone else who works under them. If the leader makes an uninformed decision, the actions will produce opposite results than what they intended. The decision must be made at the right moment and assigned to the right person to carry it out.

The central nervous system is the most delicate and complex system in a human body, but it works in harmonic sequences, which is a miracle. Any problem in this system will prompt a response from the rest of the system. In the decision-making process and assignment of tasks, the process must be smooth between the leader and his followers—any ailment in either part will cause the system to bleed.

A LEADER IS A COORDINATOR

When the brain decides, through its miraculous mechanisms, it assigns tasks to an appropriate part or organ of the body. Because most of these decisions affect human organisms, they all respond according to the decision made by the brain.

The brain delegates the work. For example, the eye sees a rose, the brain interprets the color and decodes the meaning and the pleasure that the flower brings to a person. Then the brain, according to it stored information, remembers that your wife likes roses, that she finds delights in them. Then the brain makes the decision to pick the flower and carry it to your wife. The brain assigns a task to the leg—walk near the flower; then hands pick the flower—keep your hand tight, do not drop the flower; legs, walk careful, so you do not trip until you arrive home.

After arriving home, the brain makes a command and sends it to the body—you are home now; smile; you are carrying a flower; kiss your wife and surprise her with the flower.

Now, this is a very simplified task delegation by your brain, even sometimes unconscious. So, the brain keeps record of which part does what, to make sure the entire system delights in life.

As the brain is a delegator of tasks, so is the leader. The work of a leader is to assign people work or leadership positions suiting to their capacity and abilities. To implement a decision and reap the intended fruits, the leader must assign tasks accordingly. That means, the leader studies with keen concentration to know the exact depth of his people's skills and determination to do the work. Because if the leader assigned a task to an under-equipped leader, they will reap minimal benefits. And if they assign the task to the wrong person, the subordinate might not do the task or perform contrary to the intended instructions, bringing failure to the leader.

The human brain is a trainer as well. It trains various parts of the body to work according to its vault of knowledge. The leader is the trainer of their people; a leader is a coach, a shepherd, a comforter and an encourager to his followers, so they gain those skills that will enable them to carry out their assigned tasks. This what make great leaders influential. "Being a good leader is about helping people reach their potential."[5]

You create a suitable environment for your people to learn, develop their talents help them work with others to realize their full potential.

The brain works as the bridge for all parts of the human body to work in harmony to reach a well-informed decision. If you smell something, the brain may say, "I am not sure what that is. Please, eyes, look around; there are dead mice in the house." Then after, the brain makes an informed decision that will prompt a proper action.

The leader is a bridge connecting different people/experts under his leadership, helping them fetch information to make well-informed decisions. The leader encourages his people to search out new ideas and data to help the team make a comprehensive decision that ensures that they leave no one in the entire system behind. Carrying out an uninformed decision may ruin the entire system.

A LEADER IS AN ACTION MOTIVATOR

The brain is the action motivator. When the decision has been made in the central nervous system, according to data available to the brain, the brain sends information via its agents with a proper force or motivation to the body to take action. The force or strength of the action will depend on the decision and the motivation behind the actions. If the brain sends a weak signal to the feet, the steps will be weak.

The work of a leader is to motivate and inspire his followers to take bold actions. The leader develops a strong motive in his followers; "for powerful motives increase the force of will."[6] So when they take action, they are bold and powerful to carry out the work. If the followers or the leader's motives are weak, then the outcomes will be weak as well.

The followers will act proportional to the motivation they receive from their leader through words of appreciation, faith in their potential, intrinsic expectations and through example. Followers will always rise as far as the encouragement they receive from their leader. Effective leaders learn the art of motivation, especially using their words to motivate and encourage.

A LEADER IS A VISION FORMULATOR

A brain is the vision formulator. Eyes are the window to the brain; the eye receives light, and through its optic nerves, it transmits the information to the central nervous system, which interprets the colors, then formulates a picture of what it has seen. Then you can say, "That is a window, and that is a blue car, and that is a brown suit." As one wise man said, "the wise have eyes in their heads, while the fool walks in the darkness."[7] So we see with our brain—the eyes are a medium to help the brain do its work.

The leader's work is to formulate an inspiring vision. They receive input from many eyes: their people, the environment, their spiritual eyes and books. From the accumulated knowledge, they and their followers formulate an inspiring vision, which motivates them and their people to persevere and keep working toward that picture they have set for themselves to achieve. The leader is a vision for the people; without vision, you are not a leader—just an entertainer.

A LEADER PROVIDES A SENSE OF PURPOSE TO HIS FOLLOWERS

A brain is the center of consciousness. The sense of who we are, the sense of true and false, the sense of compassion toward our fellow men and the sense of the world around us comes from our brain. Whatever you fill that void with, it will decide your attitude toward life and others. If God takes this ability from you, then you are like other wild animals.

The sense of connection to the universe, with God, angels and all the heavenly beings, can only be perceived in your brain. Your brain is so important, more than you appreciate.

The brain gives a purpose to each part of your body— the hands, the eyes, the ears or your skin—and all that makes you functions in perfect harmony, following the high purpose of life; your wellbeing and your prosperity is controlled through and by your brain.

The leader, in a large sense, is a giver of a reason for existence of a movement, an organization, a family, a church. People follow a leader who knows where they are going. That means the leaders must cultivate and nourish their purpose and the purpose of their followers. They must nurture it and communicate it through words, actions and interaction with people, and all that they do must reflect their purpose and mission.

So, when you see a society that has lost its sense of who they are, know there is a problem with its leadership. The joy and the prosperity of any community depends on the condition of the heart of its leaders and the kind of spirit that controls their actions.

RECAP | AN OVERVIEW OF LEADERSHIP

1. Leadership is essential in nurturing a well-balanced life. The prosperity of a person and a society depends primarily on effective leadership.
2. Awareness of your roles as a leader will give you clarity of thought and goals. This is the secret recipe for beginning the greatness in you.
3. Cultivating those skills that will equip you to realize the full potential of your leadership is parallelly crucial to your personal development.
4. The beginning of all learning starts with the burning desire to become the person you are dreaming in your mind.
5. Your effectiveness as a leader will depend primarily on your training and commitment, what you bring to your learning and doing.

CHAPTER 2

TRAINING GROUND

AN OPPORTUNITY TO LEARN HOW TO BECOME AN EFFECTIVE LEADER

The Lord will open an opportunity for you to be trained and to learn what it means to be an effective leader. To be a prosperous leader, you must give yourself wholeheartedly to learning and developing those faculties that will make you a successful leader and influential to those around you. One must be a follower before they may invite others to follow.

Training grounds can be a physical place, such as a university, foreign country, camp or industrial place. Also, it can be a formless situation that demands an exercise of your spiritual gifts, or it can be a circumstance—a problem that causes you to learn and adapt new skills that will make you successful in your leadership. This may include physical or psychological pain, relational difficulties, spiritual struggles, financial failures or disappointments.

A coach of a soccer team may place his players in a training ground where they can have exclusive time with their athletes. This is a physical training ground. Most sport players are placed by their trainer in special grounds or places so the coach can train them.

Why have a special training ground for your leaders?

Firstly, to detach the student from their normal life. For the student of leadership to learn the deep lessons of leadership, sometimes the teacher must place them far from home or in a foreign community from the normal environment to direct their mind to the lessons they want to impact their student.

Secondly, to separate the student from the noise of daily life that prevent them from paying attention.

Thirdly, to show the seriousness of the training. The students must know in their hearts that the training is vital for their success. So, the instructor must take him from familiarity.

Fourthly, the teacher can have one-on-one conversation with the student. Heart-to-heart conversation. It is very hard to instruct someone in the matter of importance if they are not committed to the training. Also, it's hard for the students to listen to the master if the noise of daily life clouds their minds.

Everyone is born with the seed to be an influential leader. Influence depends on the training and commitment the student brings to their training and devotion to learn from their teacher, the master. Leaders-in-making are coached by experienced leaders—

we call them masters. These are individuals who open your eyes to see the path that leads to an effective leader. That's why the person who has not learned how to learn and obey from their master is unlikely to be successful in their career.

By divine guidance, the Lord placed Daniel and his colleagues in the palace of Babylon to be trained and learn what it means to be leaders in a foreign land, at the same time as being followers of God. The circumstances that placed Daniel and his friends in Babylon were difficult. This happened after the nation of Israel was besieged by King Nebuchadnezzar, and some Israelites were taken captive to Babylon:

> Then the king ordered Ashpenaz, chief of his court officials, to bring into the king's service some Israelites. Among those who were chosen were some from Judah: Daniel, Hananiah, Mishael and Azariah. The chief official gave them new names: to Daniel, the name Belteshazzar; to Hananiah, Shadrach; to Mishael, Meshach; and to Azariah, Abednego.[8]

According to the Nebuchadnezzar's commands, they assigned the youth to the school of leadership for three years in Babylon. Remember, these were young people who were well-accustomed to the culture, governance and administration of the kingdom of Israel.

The main purpose for the king to train these young people was to be representative for him in managing his empire; some were to be governors, administrators, counselors, magicians and commanding officers. They were to learn the language of Chaldeans, the culture, the religion, the governance of Babylon, science, history, astrology and courses that would make them successful in their leadership assignments.

There were other students from conquered empires, from the lines of royalty, who joined Daniel and his friends to learn leadership. It was a school blessed with a mixture of cultures and expertise. This school can be compared to executive leadership courses offered in a university: Harvard, Stanford, West Point and other schools around the world. These are courses offered to individuals who have very stable careers, but the training is offered to give them strong wings to fly in inspiring others to achieve great things.

People who desire to develop their leadership wings accept opportunities to learn with gladness. As a leader-in-making, when an opportunity comes to attend university, do not let it pass by—attend school. These are providences that the Lord opens for you to be trained. If you are employed, and the company offers an opportunity for leadership training, jump into the courses and learn all that you can—these are opportunities that the Lord is opening for you. Attend leadership seminars, talk to experienced leaders, read leadership books. If it has passed through your eyes, pick and read; these are golden opportunities that will place you with great leaders and make you shine like stars.

Every opportunity that opens for you to develop your skill, use it with all your heart, like Daniel and his friends. They did not refuse the invitation to attend the school in Babylon, waiting for angels from Heaven to train them—they knew it was God leading.

God uses experienced leaders to train his future leaders. Joshua was trained under the leadership of Moses, Elisha was trained under the leadership of Elijah, Solomon was trained under the leadership of David. David was nurtured under the guidance of the prophet Samuel. Abraham trained Isaac. So, it's God's design that we should learn from others. If the Lord places you under the leadership of someone, whether you like them or not, learn and observe—there is wisdom in experience. Young leaders will save time and become effective in their leadership if they place themselves under the guidance of wise leaders.

While Daniel was faithfully learning science, culture, astronomy and mathematics in the school of leadership in Babylon, the Lord was training Daniel to interpret dreams and visions—the special abilities that made Daniel shine compared to the rest of his colleagues. While you gain secular training, as a faithful servant of the Lord, you should devote yourself in learning the divine oracles of God and trusting the promises of God. The privilege of communion with God will endow you with a wisdom that will manifest through you a hundred times compared to those who have only worldly training.

The greatest need of the world today is not politi-cians, scientists, doctors, preachers or engineers; though we still need them, we need individuals who have divine wisdom to carry out a hard decision solved by those connected with God more. There are complex problems that leave people of learned capabilities scratching their heads; they do not know what to do, but these are opportunities for people like you to seize and illuminate for your Master, like Daniel, Joseph, Esther and Nehemiah.

But there is another school of leadership for the sons and daughters of God—the school of hardship:

In the school of self-denial and hardship he [Moses] was to learn patience, to temper his passions. Before he could govern, he must learn to obey. His own heart must be in harmony with God before he could teach the knowledge of His will to Israel. By his own experience he must be prepared to exercise a fatherly care over all who needed his help.[9]

God sent Moses to the desert of Median to work as a shepherd for 40 years to learn how to lead himself first before leading the nation of Israel.

Every disappointment, difficulty, pain and turmoil that the world throws upon you is an opportunity to learn those qualities that will make you useful and successful. Yes, it was not comfortable for Daniel to leave his homeland and reallocate to Babylon; neither was it glory for Moses to leave metropolitan Egypt and live in the desert. These circumstances brought anguish and pain to these great men. So, will it be with us too; when problems hit us hard, it will be painful. We will find ourselves in distressing situations, not because we plan to be there, but because God may have ordained the ordeal to teach us humility. I cannot predict what will bring tears to you, but I know that the holy angels are protecting and comforting us in these situations. The Lord's care is still with us. The only need is for us to humble ourselves and learn from the Master.

The attitude of a student of leadership is that every problem, whether big or small, is a steppingstone to greatness. Leaders grow by overcoming adversity. You are being forged to strength through pain. It stretches your spiritual muscles, through trusting God in the thick of despair. Faith can only grow as it is exercised to look beyond the difficulties of today to the victory beyond hardship and self-denial. As the saying goes, "No pain, no gain." You grow and strengthen your leadership wings through flying in turbulent weather.

OTHER LEADERS WHO WERE PLACED IN A TRAINING GROUND BY GOD'S PROVIDENCE

Before God elevated Joseph to the position of prime minister in ancient Egypt, the Lord allowed Joseph to be sold to Egypt as a slave, and they also threw him into a prison because of his faithfulness. The Lord lifted him up in due time. "So, when the Midianite merchants came by, his brothers pulled Joseph up out of the cistern and sold him for twenty shekels of silver to the Ishmaelites, who took him to Egypt."[10]

The Holy Spirit sent Jesus for 40 days into the desert before he started his ministry of preaching and healing. "Then Jesus was led by the Spirit into the wilderness to be tempted by the devil. After fasting forty days and forty nights, he was hungry."[11]

Paul, before he started his apostolic ministry, was sent by God to the Arabian desert for three years to reflect on the revealed word of God and his new mission:

But when God, who set me apart from my mother's womb and called me by his grace, was pleased to reveal his Son in me so I might preach him among the Gentiles, my immediate response was not to consult any human being. I did not go up to Jerusalem to see those who were apostles before I was, but I went into Arabia. Later I returned to Damascus. Then after three years, I went up to Jerusalem to get acquainted with Cephas and stayed with him fifteen days.[12]

Abraham was caused to wander in the desert of Canaan by God. Also, God delayed blessing him with a son until old age:

The Lord had said to Abraham, go from your country, your people and your father's household to the land I will show you. So, Abraham went, as the Lord had told him; and Lot went with him. Abraham was seventy-five years old when he set out from Harran. He took his wife Sarai, his nephew Lot, all the possessions they had accumulated and the people they had gained in Harran, and they set out for the land of Canaan, and they arrived there.[13]

Sovereign Lord, what can you give me since I remain childless and the one who will inheritance] my estate is Eliezer of Damascus? And Abraham said, you have given me no children; so, a servant in my household will be my heir. Then the word of the Lord came to him: This man will not be your heir, but a son who is your own flesh and blood will be your heir. He took him outside and said, look up at the sky and count the stars if indeed you can count them. Then he said to him, so shall your offspring be.[14]

God sent Isaac to the land of Gerar to learn humility and faith:

Now there was a famine in the land besides the previous famine in Abrahams time and Isaac went to Abimelek king of the Philistines in Gerar. The Lord appeared to Isaac and said, do not go down to Egypt; live in the land where I tell you to live. Stay in this land for a while, and I will be with you and

will bless you. For to you and your descendants, I
will give all these lands and will confirm the oath I
swore to your father Abraham.[15]

God sent Jacob to his uncle Laban for about 20
years to learn the same lesson as his father Isaac and
grandfather Abraham:

*"Then Isaac sent Jacob on his way, and he went to
Paddan Aram, to Laban son of Bethuel the Aramean,
the brother of Rebek, who was the mother of Jacob
and Esau."[16]*

The children of Israel traveled through the desert
for 40 years to learn the same lessons their father
Abraham learned: faith and humility. Though most of
them, except Joshua and Caleb, failed the school:

*"The Lord your God has blessed you in all the work
of your hands. He has watched over your journey
through this vast wilderness. These forty years the
Lord your God has been with you, and you have
not lacked anything."[17]*

Moses continued to count the blessings that the
Lord performed to teach the children of Israel to love
and obey their Redeemer and King:

*Remember how the Lord your God led you all the
way in the wilderness these forty years, to humble
and test you to know what was in your heart,*

whether you would keep his commands. He humbled you, causing you to hunger and then feeding you with manna, which neither you nor your ancestors had known, to teach you that man does not live on bread alone but on every word that comes from the mouth of the Lord. Your clothes did not wear out and your feet did not swell during these forty years. Know then in your heart that as a man disciplines his son, so the Lord your God disciplines you.[18]

Before you become a person of influence, you must be willing to be humbled by God and allow him to take control of your life, so He can train you to effectively lead His people.

Daniel and other great leaders of the Bible accepted training as a steppingstone to their destination. They never murmured, though they were placed under harsh circumstances. They followed the Master with full commitment wherever He sent them, and at the end of their training, the Lord placed them in positions of power and authority to shine and represent Him in the world. "This is the aim of God to do the same to the Young men as he did to Daniel, only if they are to accept the lord's discipline. The life of Daniel and his fellows is a demonstration of what He will do for those who yield themselves to Him and with the whole heart seek to accomplish His purpose."[19] This is an open door for every person who thirsts and desires to lead and inspire the world for our Creator.

Learning demands discipline; it sometimes produces pain. Remember that always training is uncomfortable. Those who persevere during training sessions come the other end of the tunnel bathed with freshness of power and wisdom. Here are some benefits that you will gain after you patiently wait unto the Lord to fulfill his promises to you.

TRAINING HELPS YOU KNOW YOURSELF WELL AND EXPOSES YOUR CHARACTER FLAWS

Meanwhile, in the training ground, the students will appreciate their limits as human beings, and how often they need the help of God and fellow leaders. This serves the purpose of preventing the sin of self-exaltation. To lead others, you must know yourself well— what are your strengths? What are your weaknesses? — so you can correct them. What are you capable of doing yourself, and how much do you need the help of your friends?

For the leader to acknowledge with intelligence who they are, the only way is to test themselves in a crucible of life's difficulties. We measure the strength of a metal through the pressure of fire—how long it takes to melt under extreme temperature. And under the pressure of a load—how much it can withstand without bending or breaking. All these tests aid the student of leadership, to comprehend what made them and where the Master can use them so to shine, and where can they use their abilities at greater capacity.

When you are in a training ground, you realize there are things you were not created to do. These are your limits. You will never be God, and you will never do the work only God can do for you. You need to acknowledge that you are a human being and your portion is to faithfully do your assignment as the Lord has given to you.

The first lesson you will learn is that you cannot change people, so stop trying to change them. You are venturing on forbidden ground, which will produce thorns in your path, and if you're not careful, they will hamper your development.

Another thing that you may learn in training ground is that there are things that can only be done as a team, not as one person. To work with others well, you must know yourself before you appreciate others with the uniqueness of their personalities—you need an in-depth understanding of yourself. As one author said in *Psychology Today*, it is "all too easy to harshly judge others, but when we actually respond to the call of Socrates to know thyself and when we truly come to understand our subtle, intuitive mind, we become more compassionate and understanding of others."[20] Compassion connects people; the only way to connect with people is to know their needs and desires.

Sometimes, leaders task themselves heavily in doing everything themselves, so to take all the credit themselves, or out of fear that things will go wrong if delegated to other leaders. But this is a lack of training, discipline and vision. If you want to crawl like a tortoise, then you keep trying to work alone; but if you are dreaming big, envisioning flying like an eagle, training will show you that it's all about working with others in harmony to achieve great results. Like it or not, in the training ground you realize that working alone is futile and shortsighted.

TRAINING HELPS YOU MASTER YOUR MIND

Without self-control, the leader can achieve nothing or last for long. The leader is the light and hope for his followers. These responsibilities demand energy, commitment and self-command. The leader must discern when to open their mouth and when to keep quiet. The leader must control their thoughts, because he pours out springs of life to motivate his believers to achieve great things.

To continue working hard and moving toward the goals the leader has set for themselves, though the progress may grow difficult and painful. The leader must be diligent in controlling their heart; it requires considerable mental capacity to press on when the path becomes narrower and narrower.

Often, the leader will be cursed by their followers. They will murmur against them, even occasionally they may want to destroy them. These are very important and difficult moments. If the leader has not learned to control themselves during the training period, they will stumble and fall apart, and the entire organization will disintegrate. The secret of all success is self-control.

TRAINING HELPS YOU DEVELOP CHARACTER

We can only achieve character development through training. The Lord gives all the opportunities and resources for you to develop the character that will make you successful in this life and the life to come, but success depends on your personal efforts. Leaders without character are just grass that gets beaten when a storm strikes. Leaders with strong character are like rocks that stand still after the storm has passed by. Leaders exist to solve problems, to hustle with adversity. Without character, there is no leadership.

The only way the teacher will know where you are lacking is through testing and training. The reason that the greatest Teacher places you in hardship is to show you where your character is lacking and where you need help from Him, so He may support you to reach your character developments goals. If you deem there is no need for spiritual development, then why suffer? To create that desire in you, the Teacher reveals the flaws in your character development so you may partner with Him in correcting them and reach the highest advancement you ever thought possible.

Recall the story of Jesus: one day, his disciples were traveling in a boat on the lake of Galilee, and Jesus was not with them. Jesus was on shore, on the mountain, communing with his Father. His disciples were fighting for their lives against a severe storm. As they fought for their lives, Jesus came, walking on the water. When they saw him, they did not realize it was Jesus; they assumed it was a ghost. Then, Jesus said, "Do not be afraid, it is I."

Then Peter said, "If it is you, allow me to walk on the water like you," and Jesus said, "You can," and Peter stepped out of the boat, walking on the water. After a few steps, Peter took his eyes off Jesus, and he was swallowed by the waves. He cried out for help, and Jesus stretched out his hand and lifted Peter up. Jesus said, "Where is your faith?"

Through this experience, Peter's weakness was brought to light. He did not understand the working of faith that held fast to the promises of God. Instead of clinging in faith to the promise of God, he looked upon the storm, and he learned his lesson. Peter could not have learned the lesson of faith if he did not believe that Jesus would enable him to walk on the water; he would never have realized that his faith was superficial.

The only way to learn if your character is well-culti-vated is for God to place you in a training ground. In the matter of faith and spiritual growth, because our heavenly Father is our Teacher, He is the only one to place us in a training ground where our strengths will be sharpened and our weakness or shortcomings will be uncovered, so we may partner with Him in correcting them.

If you study the training of the 12 disciples, one lesson that is showed objectively is that Jesus placed his disciples in various circumstances so they may learn the nature and limitations of mankind without God. But he showed them the potential in themselves and in this world if they partnered with God. He revealed His character to them, so they may learn from Him. If there is anything that will set you free from myriad difficulties of life as you connect with people, it is to know your weaknesses, shortcomings, limitations—and your potential—wherever the Lord places you.

TRAINING HELPS YOU UNDERSTAND YOUR PURPOSE AND MISSION

While the Teacher is training you, He explains your purpose and the reason for your existence. This helps you free yourself from doubt and fear. Sometimes we get clouded by the noise of this world and get sidetracked from our path to greatness.

Humans by nature want to conform to those around them; we want to speak like everyone else, we want to eat like our friends. But these desires to conformity can cause us to forget our calling that has been laid before us by our Creator. Everyone has their own path to follow to arrive at their destiny. Failing your mission means you are following someone else's mission, which will not bring joy and fulfillment in your life.

This is the reason the Master places you in a training ground, so that you may remember and reconnect with your purpose and mission in life. If the leader does not know why they exist and what their mission is, it is just a matter of time before they will get disheartened and discouraged, and discourage their people in turn.

Moses, Joseph, Abraham and Jacob all reconnected with their purpose and mission while in training grounds. Because a training ground involves pain and discomfort, it causes you to dig deeper into your heart, to search out the real you. Then it causes you to ask questions like: Why are you here? Why were you born? Why were you created? Why are you a leader? How can you develop your skills? How can you solve this problem, that problem? We can only ask all these questions when we are under the forge of pain either emotionally, psychologically, physically or spiritually. Anyone who misses these seasons of soul searching loses opportunities to grow and develop their leadership capabilities.

It's vital to consider and reflect where things are not working right if you encounter difficult problems. Relational problems, because they touch our emotions, are the most difficult challenges to face. Most of us run from them. But if you take a moment to reflect, learn and reinvent yourself by discovering your purpose and mission in life, there will be an abundance of joy and happiness in your endeavors.

Not only that, but you will never walk in darkness, because you will connect with a divine mission, and the Lord of wisdom will counsel you on the methods and tools to use in furthering the mission passed to you by God.

The Lord appeared in the desert and Moses received his mission to lead the children of Israel to the Promised Land.

Esther reconnected with her mission to save the children of Israel from the hand of Haman. She faced the problem with prayer and courage that preserved the lives of her fellow Israelites.

Abraham received the assurance of the promise that sealed his purpose for existence while wandering in the desert.

Daniel, the man whom we have centered our discussion on, discovered his life's mission in exile in Babylon, and through challenges and problems, the Lord revealed to him His purpose by placing Daniel in the court of Babylon.

My friend, rejoice and accept the discipline of the Lord with joy, because when you come out of it, you will be a new person, inspired by a mission and purpose in your life.

TRAINING HELPS YOU REMOVE THE LIMITS FROM YOUR MIND

During training, the Lord places you under His watchful care; through high and low, He shows you the secret of his strength. God gave the power to perform miracles to Moses while he was in the desert. When Moses was wondering and doubting if the Israelites would receive him as their savior from the hand of Pharaoh, God gave him the power to perform miracles before the Israelites, Pharaoh and the Egyptians.

Daniel realized the Lord had gifted him with the ability to interpret dreams and visions while in the foreign land. It was because the king had dreams that no one could interpret, except Daniel. After the Lord revealed the secret to Daniel, he proclaimed that God is above all else.

There is so much a man can accomplish if he realizes the richness of the abilities that God has in store for each one of us. We have billions of nerve cells that need exercise to do great things. The human body is wonderful, made for and capable of doing miracles. Think about innovators like Newton, Galileo, Tesla, Boeing and many more. These were men with a passion like us but decided with all their heart to exercise the brains that God gave them.

Not even the king could comprehend the power and capacity of Daniel's brain that he could solve a mystery that no other in the kingdom could. The life of Daniel is the testimony of what men can be if they unite with God and exercise their brain to think and work. When human unites with divine power in creating services to make mankind happy and better, there is no limit to ingenuity.

The only way a leader may discover that the limits of their mind is when they are placed in a training ground. Training grounds open more opportunities and possibilities to a person than any other place. How could Abraham know that he would have a baby, when he was 100 years old? How could Joshua believe that he could command the sun and moon to stand still? Appreciate the wisdom of God to shake you, so you may realize the possibilities available for you, only if you work and believe.

TRAINING YOU HOW TO FIGHT

To be victorious in leading people, you must know how to fight battles and command soldiers. Leaders exist to subdue enemies and to win battles of life. If you have no wisdom to fight, your people are doomed. "Wisdom makes one wise person more powerful than ten rulers in a city."[21] Effective leaders are warriors— they possess the courage of lions; at the same time, they have the wisdom to navigate through life's challenging problems.

King Solomon gave another observation on the power of wisdom: "There was once a small city with only a few people in it. And a powerful king came against it, surrounded it and built huge siege works against it. Now there lived in that city a man poor but wise, and he saved the city by his wisdom So I said, Wisdom is better than strength."[22] A leader who knows how to use wisdom to win for their people has no limit on their advancement. When the Lord places you in a training ground, he wants to teach you how to gain wisdom, so wage your battle adroitly.

EQUIPPING YOU FOR YOUR ASSIGNMENT

When you're in a training ground, the Teacher blessed you with opportunities to experiment with all kinds of tools that you will use in leading people. Doctors are sent to medical school to be equipped with the knowledge and skills that they need to perform their jobs to perfection. Soldiers are sent to training camps to be equipped with tools they need in war. Without skills, a soldier is useless in a battle. Committing untrained officers to fight your battles will prove catastrophic.

God placed Daniel in the school of leadership in Babylon to be equipped with the tools he needed to carry out God's mission in the court of Babylon. He learned languages; how court proceedings were conducted; how to address the king; how to deal with the laws of Medes and Persia; how to cooperate with his friends to solve problems; and how to use science, cultures and mathematics to solve problems. All these were tools that Daniel needed to be the representative of God in that foreign country.

How could Daniel communicate with the king if he was not skilled in the language of Chadians? Yes, he may have an ability to interpret dreams, but without command of language, it would have availed nothing. You may say God would have performed a miracle and given him the ability to speak like the Babylonians; this could have gone against the character of God. From the beginning of ages, God has ordained that man should be faithful in his assigned task and leave the rest to Him.

God provided the opportunity for Daniel to develop his intelligence; Daniel cooperated with God, and he achieved wonders. As a leader, do you work and trust God to do His part; here lies the secret of all success.

IT'S NOT ABOUT YOU, BUT THE MASTER

We all have a tendency to think the work or assignment depends on us being accomplished, so we look upon our weakness and give up. But during the training phase, wherever the Lord places you, you realize that the whole thing is bigger than you. The entire universe, God and all the host of heaven are interested and directly involved with the mission. There is no need to fear but press on through faith in Jesus.

When Abraham left his native land, and the Lord appeared to him and assured Abraham his offspring would populate the entire land of Canaan, he questioned God: "How can this be, because I'm old and there are no possibilities of having a child?" But the Lord reminded him, "It is not about you, it is about what I can do for you. Keep trusting."

God placed the apostle Paul under a dilemma: he was a preacher and minister of God. But he had a weakness that was torturing him day and night, so he prayed, "Lord, can you take this thing away from me?" The Lord responded, "My grace is sufficient for you, for my power is made perfect in weakness."[23] I think this is the most powerful promise for any leader out there— God is enough for all your weaknesses. His mighty power can only be manifested through weak vessels. So, delight and rejoice in your weakness as you continue trusting in his promises.

RECAP | AN OPPORTUNITY TO LEARN HOW TO BECOME AN EFFECTIVE LEADER:

1. God uses hardships and difficult circumstances to train leaders. Leaders must accept hardships and disappointments in life as opportunities to learn and improve themselves.
2. The development of muscles is directly proportional to your discipline to exercise. The moment you stop training, your muscles shrink. It is vital as a leader to remember that training and learning is for life.
3. As a leader, you must use every opportunity that opens for you to learn how to become a successful leader, whether is going to school, reading a book or taking a leadership course.
4. Remember training reveals where you must improve. It reveals your weakness as well as your strengths. It will connect you with your mission, equip you for your life work, and you will be empowered by God's promises.

CHAPTER 3

STUDENT OF LEADERSHIP

THE QUALITIES OF A STUDENT OF LEADERSHIP

To be successful students in any subject, you need to possess those qualities that will make you an effective learner. The same principle applies in leadership development. Each one of us is born with a potential of becoming a great leader. The marked difference of those who achieve greatness in leadership development are those who possess the right attitude on leadership, wisdom to choose right calling, attractive personality and depth of learning.

THE ATTITUDE OF A STUDENT OF LEADERSHIP

Then the king ordered Ashpenaz, chief of his court officials, to bring into the king's service some of the Israelites from the royal family and the nobility.[24]

Family background can be a major factor in deter-mining your success in this world. There is a reason Nebuchadnezzar selected these young men from royalty and nobility; those born in royal families had the opportunity to learn and observe how men of authority carried out their work. They were also given opportu-nities to develop those skills that gave them advantages over common men. They were trained to think like leaders and overseers of the rest of the society.

There was no endowment in their blood or their brain, the only thing that gave them special privileges was their training. We have examples in the Bible of men born in royal lines proving to be failures and shaming the kingdom. An example is the son of David, Adonijah, who showed himself a fool by trying to take the kingdom without the blessing of his father.

The major deciding attribute between those who become great leaders and those end up being led by others is their mental attitude toward life and leadership. David came from a very poor family, but he became a very powerful leader because of his attitude toward life: he believed in the mighty power of God—the Leader of all and Creator of all. David allowed the mighty God to control his mind. The power of God knows no limits or boundaries. So, the family that raises its children in the fear of the Lord and His power will rule the world forever.

If the deciding attribute for those who become great leaders in the careers of their choice is their mental attitude, their frame of mind. How can you change your thinking to prepare yourself for greatness? To learn this process, we will examine some lives of great men in the Bible and how God changed their perspectives about life and responsibilities.

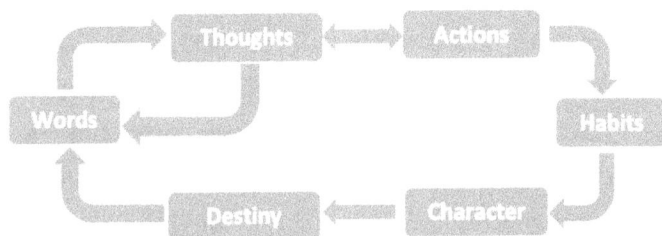

The beginning of great changes in your life begins with words. Refer to the figure above. When a child is born, they have no thoughts of their own, but they form their perspective about life according to what they see, feel, hear, smell and taste. So, their brain is empty, ready to receive anything that is poured into it. If they receive words of encouragement and love, that is what will shape their thoughts. If the words that they receive are negative and discouraging, those are the kind of thoughts will form in their brain.

Words are life, and words are a power that can destroy or give life. King Solomon once said, "the tongue has the power of life and death, and those who love it will eat its fruit."[25] Solomon here affirms this truth; after a period of study and observation of the power of words, watch your words, because they have the power to give life and bring death.

Jesus commented on the power of words: "the Spirit gives life; the flesh counts for nothing. The words I have spoken to you them are full of the Spirit and life."[26] What Jesus is saying here is that words I speak to you have the Spirit of God, and the Spirit of God gives life and power. If you want to have an abundance of life, preserve your life and the life of others; change the words you hear and speak. Through words, God created the world and everything therein. We create the world around us with our words. "From the fruit of their mouth, a person's stomach is filled; with the harvest of their lips they are satisfied."[27] As leaders-in-making, we watch our words, pay attention to what we hear, read and speak.

When you firmly decide to think like a leader, the initial step is to change your words, especially what you feed your brain. This includes the movies you watch, pictures you see, books you read, music you listen to and conversations that you engage in on a daily basis. There is a connection between your words and your thoughts; your words shape your thoughts, and your thoughts formulate your words. We become what we think about.

The thoughts that you nurture in your brain are the source of great actions. As Doctor Amen said, "Your thoughts affect every cell in your body."[28] The cells in your body produce the energy that you need to perform powerful actions. The more you think about something, the more your brain develops new pathways and cements them in your brain. In other words, your nervous system expands to accommodate the intensity of your thoughts, and it will increase the power of your actions.

But not every thought that comes to your brain should be accepted as a truth. If you exercise your ability to think correctly, some thoughts must be rooted out and some must not be accepted. People plant thoughts through their behaviors toward you; if what they are throwing at you is not healthy and encouraging, refuse them by replacing them with good thoughts.

God changed Abraham's thoughts from scarcity to abundance by asking him to look up to the sky and count the stars; if he could count them, that is how many his descendants would be.[29] Remember, when the Lord was telling Abraham to do this, Abraham was a childless old man. But the Lord wanted Abraham to change his thoughts, to think bigger than his limited mind. The Lord wanted Abraham to have His mind. The mind of God is higher than ours. If we allow Him to rule in our hearts, our thoughts will be big, according to His promises in His Word.

The Lord used a picture to change the thoughts of His servant. As a leader, why not draw a picture of what kind of leader you want to become? Look upon it, in the morning and the evening. You want to focus your brain to what you intend to become rather than what you do not have.

Sometimes, God uses dreams to alter our limited mind to unlimited possibilities in His promises. When Jacob was fleeing from his brother Esau, he was filled with thoughts of despair and fear—yes, he had gotten the blessings he wanted by cheating. But his mind was suffering from guilt and negative thoughts about himself and the future—that he would not succeed. But the Lord was merciful to him; He changed his thoughts by giving him a dream of angels descending and ascending from the throne of God.[30] This changed Jacob's mind from fear to assurance and courage.

In another account, God gave a dream to young Joseph, that one day, he would be the ruler of the house of the Lord.[31] The dream came to be fulfilled after many years. God allowed this to happen, according to his divine purpose, to elevate the thoughts of this young man, so he could carry himself according to the promise. The moment your thoughts are changed from thinking small to thinking big, your entire perspective on life, opportunities, hardship and disappointments takes a new turn.

Leaders dream noble and big goals. One famous author said, "remember that you will never reach a higher standard than you yourself set. Then set your mark high."[32] It all begins with thoughts.

Thoughts and actions are interchangeable; your actions influence your thoughts. Your actions should be in harmony with your thoughts. If you want to be happy, act happy, and do those things that will make you happy, like picking beautiful flowers, singing happy songs, helping a friend, volunteering or reading a book that lifts your thoughts high.

Every time you affirm your thoughts by actions, you are telling your brain to store those thoughts for future use. Some works of a leader are serving others in a different capacity to achieve their dreams; then, as a leader-in-making, help them. This will affirm your desire to be a leader. Works are a blessing given to us by God. By working to put those talents He has given to us to use, we are influencing our brain to think high.

Sometimes, we think small because of fear, and the only way to conquer fear is action. When you act to change what you were afraid of, it changes your thoughts. You may think, "I'm not capable of running 10 kilometers," but if you put yourself to work, you will surprise yourself and run 20 kilometers. Leaders become influencers because of their actions; they think, speak and act. Put yourself to work and never take counsel from your fearful thoughts—that is why it is vital to feed your brain with the Word of God, that your actions become bold and powerful. The more you repeat an action, it built habits.

Habits produce greatness. If you do a great deed once, and that's it, the fruit dies. Leaders keep working, repeating those life-giving acts, and keep reinventing themselves to improve those deeds. The goal of a leader is to repeat actions over and over, so they may strengthen the new pathway in their brain. Every time you engage in a new action, your brain creates a new pathway in the nerves through electrical imprints. The more you do, the longer those memories stay.

Creating new habits requires the strength of the will and the mental toughness to stay on the course. God has given the ability to each one of us to choose and exert the power of the will to accomplish these decisions. The power of the will is strengthened through exercise; every time you decide and act on your decision, it strengthens the power of your will. The more you work, the stronger it becomes.

Without persistence, you will diverge from the course. Sometimes you will be discouraged, but keep working. On other occasions, your actions will not bear the fruits you intended, but you must keep your spirit high.

Creating new habits is not an easy task; that's why God has never left us alone. When you unite your will with the will of God, nothing will ever be impossible for you. Seeking God's strength in prayer while developing new habits will give you the strength to keep working toward your goals. Habits form character. The goal of a leader is to nurture beautiful character that resembles the likeness of God.

Character makes you influential. Character will make you a magnet to attract followers. Character becomes who you are, inside-out. Now your actions are in harmony with your thoughts and your thoughts are in harmony with actions.

Your character will decide your destiny. Destiny is the picture you have set for yourself and your followers to achieve. The goal for the leaders is to achieve their visions.

The vision influences the words of a leader, and their words shape their thoughts, and their thoughts are guided by their spiritual wisdom, and their thoughts manifest themselves in actions. Repeated actions form habits. Character is formed through habits. Character makes the leader, who determines their destiny.

CHOOSING THE CALLING THAT USES YOUR STRENGTHS, TALENTS AND GIFTS

The other quality King Nebuchadnezzar ordered the chief of Eunuchs to look for when choosing students for the school of leadership was that they must be **"young men without physical defects."** In the time of Nebuchadnezzar's kingship, the people representing the king were to be physically and mentally fit.

This requirement was placed by the king because there were tasks that needed those who were performing them to be physically fit; for example, if you want to be a fighter pilot, you must have a good vision. If you're working in construction areas, you may be required to have all your hands and feet to do the task. Does it mean you cannot be a leader if you are handicapped? The answer is no. Everyone, no matter their limitations, can be leaders in the profession of their choice (in the area they are gifted).

The very important lesson here is to choose the right profession that makes you happy and feel gifted. Your talent may look small, but develop it as much as you can, because great things start small. Place yourself in the area where you believe your abilities will be well-used. Study your strengths and your limits; this will open doors to opportunities that you never thought existed and will help you avoid investing your energy and time on things that will give you small returns. We must learn how to invest our scarce resources only to those fertile ventures; this may be a factor between high achievers and mediocre achievers.

You may say, "Now I have been employed in an area that is not suitable for my talents." This may be correct because we need to live. Many times, we start from the lowest point in life, and then we grow to the highest position in life. As I study and research very successful leaders in history, most of them developed their gifts in their spare time.

When you are employed, those eight hours do not belong to you; they belong to your employer. You act according to their vision. So, out of 24 hours, you have 16 hours remaining. Minus eight hours of sleep, and you have eight hours remaining. In these eight hours, at least set apart two hours every day to do things you love and cultivate your talents. The day you least expect it, they will be called to use, and that may be your breakthrough.

It is paramount to know your gifts and your limits. Cultivate your gifts as best you can, even if you feel they are small, invest in them—big trees grow out of small seeds. Even if you're faithful in small ways, the Lord will trust you with more.

To choose the right career that uses your talents, you must identify the talents gifted to you by your Creator at birth: "At your birth a seed is planted. That seeds are your uniqueness. It wants to grow, transform itself, and flower to its full potential. It has a natural, assertive energy to it. Your life's task is to bring that seed to flower, to express your uniqueness through your work. You have destined to fulfill."[33]

Talent is all that the Lord has endowed you to live happy, bless others and fulfill His purpose for you. Talents include health, wealth, time, strength, natural resources, knowledge, friends. These are general talents that are given to all of us, according to His great wisdom. The question that all of us must answer before our Creator is how did we invest them to bless His work and mankind? God expects us to invest every gift that He has bestowed to us and expects a return from His investment.

Each one of us have been given special abilities that are unique compared to others, for services to our fellow people. Here are words of wisdom from Robert Greene in his book, *Mastery*: "It is there already within you. You have nothing to create; you merely need to dig and refind what has been buried inside of you all along."[34] These special abilities open doors for us to find our careers for life. Your goal as a leader-in-making is to discover your unique gifts that God has given you and labor with all your mighty to place yourself in the right place to use them. The more you develop them, the more you will be given.

I have few suggestions on how to discover your unique abilities (talents):

1. What brings true joy to your heart? If you answer this question well, it will open doors to your natural abilities. "We are born with innate desires and abilities that bring fulfillment as we develop them."[35] Each brain is created uniquely; the nervous system of each one of us is wired differently, and the wiring determines what brings true joy to you.

2. List all the activities you do that make you creative. List them in order of how they influence you and others. "Your work then is something connected deeply to who you are, not a separate compartment in your life."[36] Normally, your natural abilities will push you to be creative and do more. Work is the revelation of who you are inside. If your work gives you a voice to express your inner strength and influence others to live better and adopt better habits, that is your calling. Pay attention.

3. What are your childhood dreams? As a child, you spoke from your heart. Normally, these aspirations have great connections with your spiritual power and God. If you are wondering what your gifts are,

rewind back. What were your childhood dreams? Sometimes, our childhood dream job may not be your adult career, but searching out your childhood aspiration will give you a clue of what your true gifts are.

4. What occupies your mind and your thoughts more than anything else? Be very careful as you answer this question, because some of our thoughts have been corrupted by the voices of the world. The unique gifts that are buried inside of you are constantly trying to come out to bless the world and bring true joy to you.

5. Which activities, even if you endure hardship, keep you motivated to press on? Without passion, it is hard to keep fighting, when the path becomes narrower and narrower.

6. Pay attention to the inner voice that keeps pushing you to pursue your dreams. Graham Stedman, speaking on your inner voices said, "it is stoking that fire inside us that keeps us moving toward our potential, that keeps us alert to the surrounding possibilities that will help us reach our promise."[37] Our spirit keeps speaking to us, telling us of who we are and where we should go, and many times, it is the mighty Spirit of God that is trying to direct us where we should invest our energy and time.

7. Pray to God to bring you in touch with your work. Work will fill a great space in your life; working

where your talents are used will bring boundless joy to your heart, even if you are making little money.

The benefits of discovering your talents and serving in your calling

1. Your star will shine brighter and brighter. Every time you put your talent to use and cultivate it is like removing clouds in the sky to let stars visibly shine for the happiness of mankind. Remember, your star is hidden in you—let it shine. The world will see it and come to behold your glory, gifted to you by your Creator.

2. The more you use your talent; your happiness level increases. Your happiness is directly connected to your service in love and passion. Your natural abilities are not different from the gift of speech or the ability to eat—when you eat food, you feel pleasure. So, does using your talent bring pleasure.

3. The more you use your talent, the more it helps you see the meaning of life. Your God-given purpose will be clear to you.

4. The moment you discover your talents and commit to developing them, the world opens with resources waiting for you to use them. Most of us complain, "I don't have capital," or "I miss that," but the moment you are sure of who you are and your potential, the world has various resources for you to advance.

5. Men and women who develop their talents live longer. They tend to take care of their bodies, which is another talent from their Creator.

6. You will be wealthy, according to God's grace and mercy upon you. If you plant one seed of corn, given that you take care of the seed, God will shower His favor upon you. You have a guarantee of harvesting 30, 40 or 100 seeds of corn. Now, you are wealthier compared to when you started. You know God is an Investor who has invested in us, so we may return a hundred-fold to His glory. Every investor will do everything possible to reap a return from his investment; if this is the case for fallible men, how much will our Creator enable us to succeed in our investment? The Lord will do everything He can to make us fruitful; that is why He sent His only begotten son, to ensure the success of his investment. Remember the parable of the talents in Matthew 25; it is worth reading.

7. It is a miracle when you discover your unique ability and commit to develop it. Your focus becomes a laser beam. You focus your mind, resources and time to ensure that you are successful. Here is the secret for time management: passion in your investment.

8. The moment you're passionate about your talents, you have a burning desire to develop them. Connect with the right individuals to help you realize your dream. People will help individuals passionate about their work, who know where they are heading.

AN APTITUDE TO LEARN ALL
KINDS OF KNOWLEDGE

We are living in a world that changes dramatically and presents new challenges and problems that require new ways of learning, thinking and processing ideas. A leader who will be successful and influential must be open-minded to learn from all branches of knowledge and perspectives. Also, they must learn the art of listening to draw insights from other leaders.

King Nebuchadnezzar understood this principle; the young men joining the school of leadership were to have an attitude of open minds: **"showing an aptitude for every kind of learning."** No wonder the Babylonian empire was blessed with various discoveries in mathematics, astronomy, construction, trade, and irrigation—their open-minded leaders learned from different disciplines.

Abraham Lincoln, the 16th president of the United States of America, once said, "All I have learned, I learned from books."[38] President Lincoln never attended college, but through sheer power and strength to read books, and through practice, he became an expert in the law. Through his determination and hard work, he became the president of the United States of America. During his leadership, he led the nation through severe civil war—if not for his wisdom, there would be no United States of America.

Leaders are problem solvers, and problems come in different forms and shapes. To be solved, they require a leader to have vast knowledge from various branches of learning. Yes, the leaders must focus on mastering subjects of their choice, but at the same time, they must widen their learning.

Isaac Newton was a physicist with an open mind to learn. One day, as he was sitting under an apple tree, he saw an apple fall to the ground and asked, "Why did it not go up, instead came down?" That was the beginning of the discovery of gravitational force. The force that affects our lives in magnitude, that we cannot comprehend as mortal men. So, if you are a psychologist, it does not hurt to learn about music; if you a preacher, you will benefit by learning laws and business. Every subject that we learn relates to other subjects. Knowledge is not a narrow path, but a web of a good deal of other knowledge.

Solomon was the wisest man who ever lived. He was honored and respected in the world because of his broadness of knowledge. The Lord opened his heart to learn from his creations: from wild animals, people, plants, rocks and seasons. As he was absorbed in learning and searching the hidden secret of wisdom in God's created works, his mind was enlightened with God's wisdom. Every place, every experience, every element the leader encounters is the classroom.

We love the teachings of Jesus Christ because he related spiritual principles with a common experience of life. Jesus shared stories that bear great principles of God's kingdom. He shared with his audience parables that required them to exercise their minds to understand. He revealed invisible wisdom with visible elements of life. Every idea relates to another idea. This helps the leader to examine the problem from different angles and perspectives.

This means we must be open to other people's ideas and perspectives. Every person has been given his own private mind. The Lord reveals Himself to each one of us in many ways. A wise leader listens with keen mind to learn from other leaders, and from their followers. Different minds coming together at a table bring new and innovative ideas. If you want to be a great leader, you must open your mind to learn from great leaders and ordinary leaders.

THE POWER OF A PLEASING PERSONALITY

The next quality that the King Nebuchadnezzar ordered his chief of staff to look for in choosing students for the school of leadership was that they must be **"handsome"** or **"well favored."**

To understand this concept, let us go back in time to when the children of Israel wanted a king. They requested a king who looked like the neighboring kings, and in their minds, they were thinking of someone tall, big, masculine and rich; these were the qualities they were looking for in choosing their leader. God gave them exactly what they wanted—he gave them Saul. Scripture records about him that "he stood among the people, he was a head taller than any of the others. Samuel said to all the people, 'Do you see the man the Lord has chosen? There is no one like him among all the people.'"[39] At first, he looked powerful, but in a short time, he proved to be arrogant, cowardly, impatient, self-centered and disobedient.

After all this, the prophet Samuel cried unto the Lord. Then the Lord said to Samuel, "I have chosen another man to replace Saul who is humble in heart." Then Samuel anointed David, and this was said about David: "I have seen a son of Jesse [David] the Bethlehemite who is skillful in playing [instrument], a man of valor, a warrior, prudent [sensible] in speech, and a man of good presence; and the Lord is with him."[40] These qualities make you desirable to be in the presence of this man.

Men are creatures of the senses; they are attracted to the things they see, touch, smell and feel, yet they cannot understand the depth of them. The appearance of mysteriousness is powerful and attractive; anyone who desires to be a leader must possess this gift.

Habits that will increase your attractiveness:

Your vibrant health gives your followers the atmosphere of life and self-control, which is infectious. Young David was healthy and full of energy. Outward beauty can make you instantly attractive, but if the person is not proportionally built up and full of the energy which inspires actions, the charm vanishes. Health can be achieved by each one of us, no matter your circumstance. If you eat healthy, get good sleep and exercise, you live with your fellow men in harmony and peace. Your body will be healthy.

Happy individuals radiate beauty and serenity. There is power in people at peace in their heart. You can achieve this if you manage your life well. The causes of unhappiness in most of us are stress, bitterness, grief, unresolved conflict, selfishness, laziness and unbalanced health. What is inside you emits power and reveals itself in your daily interaction with people. The important work of yours as a leader-in-making is to cultivate a pure spirit. Nothing compares with purity of heart and mind. How can you develop this kind of habit? Forgive without conditions, love with all your heart, resolve conflicts as much as you can, sleep with a light heart, manage your financials, read good books, obey the Word of God and be willing to serve others with gladness and joy.

Individuals who feel secure and confident about themselves offer to people an aura of peace and tranquility. Confidence is a source of passion and vitality in the life of a leader. Confidence is power. Confidence attracts and inspires people to follow your lead. Sources of confidence for a leader include courage to act despite their fear and doubt, clinging firm to the promises of God and understanding their abilities and weaknesses in depth. Also, the leaders who have established that their purpose is to serve others have confidence in their actions. Knowledge and commitment to your purpose for life magnetizes your followers. As a student of leadership, you must cultivate confidence and invest in yourself so people feel secure around you.

You must dress appropriately and adapt to the occasion for an ambiance of beauty and wonder. There is a season for everything in life. Because people are following you, your teachers will delight greatly to see you are adaptable. Life changes constantly, and those who are rigid are not suitable for leadership development. Every situation demands your creativity. The ability to use your mind to persuade and inspire others according to the situation is vital for your leadership development and influencing others.

Individuals who pay attention and listen with a sympathetic heart are very attractive and seductive in nature, and it draws us to them. Talking too much can reduce your attractiveness. People crave being heard and understood. People want to share their stories and experiences, and they are constantly searching not just for a listening ear, but for empathy. People want to know that you are listening and care for their ideas and opinions, despite their shortcomings and status. As a student of leadership, it is mandatory to cultivate humbleness of heart to listen to your Master. Your work is not to air your ideas, but to learn from Him, to absorb every lesson He passes to you.

Good cardio helps the body circulate blood through the veins and gives the body a reddish color, which projects power and stamina (tuning the muscles). I cannot understate the importance of exercise. You must keep yourself active. Breathing fresh air and exercising your entire body will give you a beauty that cannot be bought from anywhere. Spending a few minutes every day exercising will enhance your attractiveness.

We are attracted to individuals generous in their praises and appreciation. Criticizing people will take you nowhere. People delight to have their egos lifted. Praise their hard work, their busyness, the speech they delivered, their effort to impact their communities, and appreciate them for who they are. People will love you, especially if you do it from a pure heart.

We respect individuals who know how to speak with wisdom and understanding. Speech is the most powerful gift given to mankind, so if you know how to use it, it will earn you favor and privileges. We will discuss this topic in detail in later chapters.

Men and women who are overshadowed with the favor of the Lord are romantic and powerful. If you want to inspire people for pure and noble purposes, allow God to rule in your life. He will pour his favor on you, and you will prosper wherever you go. The Lord will touch people uniquely, in so much that they will open their hearts to you.

Finally, my friends, to be very influential leaders, you must possess an attractive personality, and we can achieve this with the combination of beauty of heart, good health and a good attitude toward life and people. So, those who aspire to be leaders, pay closer attention to your personality. You can be very educated and well-endowed with physical stature, but if your personality is not well-cultivated to be a blessing to others, you will not go far.

WELL-INFORMED | SHARPEN THE AXE

Another quality that King Nebuchadnezzar put forward for the chief of staff to look for while choosing students to attend the school of leadership in Babylon was that they be **"well-informed,"** also defined as **"knowledgeable"** or **"up-to-date."**

An individual who is well-informed is a person who understands a specialized subject deeply from all perspectives. A well-informed person is an expert in his profession. To be an expert is to have a deep understanding and insight of a problem, subject or specialization.

Some experts say that it takes 10,000 hours of commitment to be a master in any specialization. The only way an individual becomes well-informed is from devotion to reading, praying, observing, learning and meditating on the subject. The ability to devote yourself to learning, working and searching for information from other experts and spending ample time understanding the subject, step by step, will give you wisdom in designing better solutions.

A deep understanding of a problem requires time, energy, devotion, discipline, reading, prayer, research, experiments and skills to connect all the veins that lead to the center of the problem you are trying to solve or understand. President John F. Kennedy once said, "leadership and learning are indispensable to each other."[41] The world changes every day, and we invent new means of solving problems. Leaders must focus on learning those skills.

Remember, leadership comes on top of your profession. Leadership gives you wings to prosper in your specialization. Before you become a great leader, you must choose a field that fits your talents and gifts and become a master in that profession. Without specialized knowledge, your leadership development will fail. Sharpen your axe.

Being informed does not mean that you gain all possible information out there, but it means you know where to get information easier and faster when you need to solve a problem. As a professional in your area of choice, it's a wise habit to study and know which person to call or to connect with to gain the information you need. Time is paramount in the life of a leader; you save time by consulting experts to gain the vital information that you need.

QUICKNESS OF UNDERSTANDING

This was another quality required by Nebuchadnezzar for the students who were to be admitted into the school of leadership in Babylon. The ability to **"quickly understand the problem."**

An individual who understands problems quickly is a person who has developed the ability to pay attention to the smallest details in order to understand the problem. Time is money, as most investors say, so a person who can solve a problem quickly and efficiently is an asset.

Habits that will enhance an individual to understands problems quickly:

Habitually pay attention to small details in solving a problem. Every problem you encounter in your life or career is a compound of small problems. A leader must have the ability to follow the chain of events from the smallest to the most obvious problem. Many times, many problems happen because of negligence in paying attention to small details. We humans tend to jump onto things or to hurry in solving problems, only to add to the existing difficulties.

A person who has been trained how to think correctly will solve any difficult problem. Most people are trained to act and speak, but few know the power of analytical thinking. To understand problems quickly, you must train your brain to think and concentrate its power on one thing at a time, try to relate it with a different aspect of the problem, while trying to understand. Thinking requires time. One leader wrote, "you need to schedule time to think, the same way you schedule time for meetings, or for dinner with a family or a friend. As a leader it must be your priority to plan and schedule quality time to exercise your brain to thinks."[42] I recommend as you are thinking on the problem, have pen and paper around you; jot every idea that pops into your mind, and rethink until you refine it. Ideas need refining, and when the idea is ready you, you will know it.

A person who is healthy physically and mentally will assimilate information quickly—your body works as one unit. If your foot is giving you pain, your brain will not work efficiently. If your nervous system lacks the necessary mineral to operate at its capacity, the brain will not receive the information it needs to understand and solve a problem. If your blood system is not circulating blood efficiently to every part of the body, your brain will not receive air and calories to work efficiently.

As a leader, you must take care of your body. Feed it well, exercise and avoid drugs. As you advance in leadership training, you will realize that the amount of food you eat and when you eat will either enhance your brain function or hinder your ability to process information. This concurs with one executive, who said, "To stay on your game, you have to be the boss of your brain and mealtimes not the other way around."[43] You must pay attention to your spiritual and physiological well-being. If you realize that there are spiritual issues to be taken care of, do so and manage them properly; if you realize that there are psychological or social issues, take care of them. Peace of mind is necessary in dealing with issues that require your full attention.

Peace of mind and tranquility of soul are the sources of vitality and strength to deal with problems as they come to our lives. To cultivate a peaceful mind is to engage in activities that promote peace. As much as possible, live with people in harmony to avoid conflict. Constantly engaging in fighting wears the body and mind. A mind that is weak cannot comprehend critical knowledge needed to solve problems.

A man who knows how to relax and rest his brain and body tends to see problems with clarity. We must learn to shut off our brains. The importance of this is that, during deep relaxation, your brain channels its energy to process information, storing it, associating it with other conjoining ideas, which is vital in creating solutions.

Your brain works by associating information. This is critical because it happens when you're relaxed. It requires discipline to accomplish this task, but if you want to create a new thing, let your brain go through its way of processing information as its Designer created. Deep sleep is critical too—when we are sleeping, our brain works hard to arrange and store information for the long term; more importantly, your brain creates the reality of the ideas you planted in your brain.

This is the reason you have dreams. When you search out, you realize that they are related with something you saw, read or heard about. Not only that, your mind tries to create a picture of what will be if that idea was put to action. Those who have a purity of thought will advance to create amazing solutions.

The most important benefit of relaxing your brain and body, and getting deep sleep, is, as you read in Scripture, divine agents communicate with us. Great prophets and leaders in the Bible received visions and dreams that shaped the history of mankind for generations, some for eternity, during deep sleeps. Daniel and King Nebuchadnezzar received dreams of great significance when they were sleeping or relaxing.

Learning how to learn is the most vital habit that every student of leadership must gain. There are many techniques and tools to learn new information and ideas. Every day, there is a new problem, challenge or opportunity that requires reinventing yourself. That means you must learn and unlearn and learn new ideas. Never allow your brain to be stagnant—learn new things every day. This habit will enhance your ability to solve difficult problems.

Maintain a conducive environment to enhancing your ability to think clearly. It is vital that you place yourself where there are minimal distractions to concentrate all your energy on dealing with the issues at hand. To achieve clarity of thought requires thinking objectively without background noise. When you are dealing with critical problems, be in a place that has enough oxygen, nice smell, ample room to stretch, even possibly to walk around. Sometimes a good view can increase clarity of thought, too.

READY AND WILLING TO SERVE

Students of leadership must serve others with humbleness of heart. The motive for a leader is to serve others, to make their lives better and worth living. This is the ultimate motive for leadership.

After the death of Solomon, his son Rehoboam took the reign of leadership, and people came to Rehoboam and said, "Your father put a heavy yoke on us, but now lighten the harsh labor and the heavy yoke he put on us, and we will serve you."[44] Rehoboam sought wisdom from elders, the men who had led the nation of Israel with his father; and they answered, "If today you will be a servant to these people and serve them and give them a favorable answer, they will always be your servants."[45]

But Rehoboam was not pleased with the idea, so he rejected the advice of the elders, and he asked for advice from the youth he grew up with, and they counseled him tell the people, "My little finger is thicker than my father's waist. My father laid on you a heavy yoke; I will make it even heavier. My father scourged you with whips; I will scourge you with scorpions."[46]

When all Israel saw that the king refused to listen to them, they answered the king, "What share do we have in David, what part in Jesse's son? To your tents, Israel! Look after your own house, David!"[47] In the aftermath of this, the kingdom was divided into two nations: North and South.

Jesus counseled his disciples that "Anyone who desires to be a great leader among you must be the servant of all." You lead because you will work hard to provide a service that people need. To be great, you must go the extra mile every time you are providing service to your people. Many companies or organizations are looking for individuals willing to go the extra mile to make their customers happy.

President John F. Kennedy spoke great words of wisdom when he was giving his first inauguration speech: "Ask not what your country can do for you, but what you can do for your country."[48] This statement is priceless. This is the essence of personal leadership. Your goal as a leader is not to look for luxury and pleasure. You're looking for an opportunity to serve and to be used in creating value in the lives other people.

Leaders are value creators. People love leaders and follow them because of the value they create for their followers. When you consider the work of John F. Kennedy, you will agree that he lived to make America great. His desire was to create value and add greatness to American society.

Another quality put forth by Nebuchadnezzar for the students of leadership was **"qualified to serve in the king's palace."** Another Bible translation says that "they must be able to stand before the King." You can have all the qualities we mentioned prior but still found to be lacking in this area.

First, a person serving at an assigned position must have the willingness to serve. The men standing before the king were required to have humbleness of spirit to serve and go where the call demanded without reservation. There are many intelligent and wealthy individuals who are not humble in spirit to serve others with humility of heart.

You see, the failure of Rehoboam's leadership was his reluctance to serve his people with humility of heart. Remember, these young people, Daniel and his friends, were to represent the king in leading his empire; how difficult could it be if he chose men who created division among the people like Rehoboam, instead of serving them and bringing peace and unity among them? The king knew what he was doing, choosing young leaders who were humble in spirit. Leadership development without humbleness and a willingness to serve is doomed from the beginning.

The men who were to stand before the king should be able to keep a secret as demanded by their master. Having a partner who is leaking secrets with the outside world is like having a leaking bucket. If the job requires people who keep secrets, then do not choose those who have a problem keeping secrets.

Most importantly, the men who were to serve the king were supposed to have the skills needed to perform their task as required by the king. That is why

Daniel and his friends where trained in literature, science, astronomy, record keeping, laws, politics and governance. Choose men who have the set of skills that will help them perform their tasks effectively.

RECAP | THE QUALITIES OF A STUDENT OF LEADERSHIP:

1. A student of leadership must accept, with humbleness of heart, training under the leadership of well-experienced leaders.
2. Students of leadership must develop a burning desire to be a leader; this must be their goal.
3. Students of leadership must identify their talents and develop them to the highest level possible.
4. Students of leadership must cultivate an attractive personality.
5. Students of leadership must have an aptitude to all kinds of learning; be open-minded.
6. Students of leadership must sharpen their talents; they must become an expert in the area of their choice.
7. Students of leadership must cultivate and nurture quickness in understanding.
8. Students of leadership must be willing and ready to serve others (ready to add value).

CHAPTER 4

PERSONAL LEADERSHIP

THE STARTING POINT TO GREATNESS

The starting point for a leader before venturing into leading others, must be to put their house in order. On the *Harvard Business Review* website, Peter F. Drucker comments on personal leadership: "now, most of us, even those of us with modest endowments, will have to learn to manage ourselves. We will have to learn to develop ourselves. We will have to place ourselves where we can make the greatest contribution."[49] This means you must cultivate your personal leadership before leading others; you must lead yourself effectively. Your private life will determine your public life. Your private victory will provide a foundation for your public victory.

Every great leader that I have read their biography or encountered have a common denominator: they are very disciplined in their personal lives. Take Mahatma Gandhi: he influenced and helped the people of India to gain their independence from the British through his self-control. Because of self-control and determination, the people followed him through thick and thin until they achieved their mission.

What about Jesus Christ? The wisdom and self-control that ruled his life were a demonstration of his well-cultivated personal life. When you read through the Gospels, you see Jesus waking early to pray and fasting. Even during his death at the cross, he maintained his relationship with his Father and still loved his enemies and prayed for them. This would not be possible if his private life was in disorder. As a leader, you cannot compensate the hard work needed to discipline yourself with anything. This is a dearest cost you must pay first, before you endeavor to persuade others to follow you.

The success that Daniel achieved during his leadership in the Babylonian court was a testimony to his well-cultivated personal leadership. He solved difficult problems because he was a well-rounded person; he was self-educated, and as a result, the prophecy he received from Heaven was the outcome of his relationship with God.

We will study Daniel's personal leadership and how we can apply his principles to our lives. Remember, true leadership principles are intricately connected with God and are unchangeable. The principles were the same during the lives of Daniel, Jesus and Paul and are the same with us today: solid values, the power of prayer, the influence of mutual friends, special abilities, proactive minds and the power of the Holy Spirit are invaluable to us today and forever.

CHOOSING PERSONAL VALUES

But Daniel resolved not to defile himself with the royal food and wine, and he asked the chief official for permission not to defile himself this way.[50]

There comes a time when a leader must decide what kind of person they want to become. A leader is defined by what kind of values they establish to live by; these are foundational blocks for the stamina and strength of their leadership.

Daniel resolved to obey God and hold fast to the principles of the kingdom of Heaven; these values determined how he processed information and decided. Daniel established his leadership values early on during his youth and training, so, later in his professional life, deciding was easy for him, because his values system was clear and decisive.

Value is what you are willing to pay for. For example, if you want to buy a Mercedes Benz worth $40,000, you agree to pay that amount of money. The value of that car is $40,000. So, in every value you establish in your life, there is a cost associated with it.

Jesus once talked about the cost of discipleship. He gave a parable: suppose you want to build a house. The first thing you do is calculate the cost of building the house, to see if you have enough resources to complete the project. If you start a foundation and do not finish the house, you will be a fool. Or, if you are a king, before you invade another kingdom, you will sit down and calculate the cost before you strike; you will be destroyed if you miscalculate. A leader must calculate the cost—he must pay for the principle that he is developing in his life.

Going back to our example of a car: the moment you pay the price, the car is yours. It starts giving you value back—comfort, transportation, durability, safety and maybe, at the end of its life, the return on investment. The reasons that you have to establish solid values at the beginning of your leadership training are that values help channel your resources; they help your followers know where you are taking them; they give credibility among fellow leaders and followers; they ease decisions, where to say yes and where to say no; they manage your time; they develop a vision and mission; they choose friends and partners.

Values are your guidepost to your destination; without them, you will miss the mark—you will never achieve your mission and vision. Let's examine some foundational values established by Daniel:

Firstly, Daniel considered his body to be the temple of the Holy Spirit, so he resolved with all his heart and might not to defile it by any means. This is a very crucial point—the medium by which the Holy Spirit may communicate with us is through our hearts and spiritual mind that dwells in our physical body, so anything that ruins the body also ruins your spiritual strength. That's why eating right is very important.

The animals which were offered at the table of the king were first dedicated to the gods of Babylon and were not killed as described in the laws of Moses. Some of these animals were not clean, so sharing this food at the table of the king was to disobey the laws of God; anyone who destroys the temple of God, God will destroy too.

Daniel put his life at stake by requesting not to defile himself with the food from the king's table. Daniel understood the power of personal leadership early on; he chose what values he would live by for the rest of his life.

Secondly, Daniel resolved to obey God; this principle is proven by his life dedicated to serve his fellow men, serving God with all his heart and his reverent prayers—he was ready to lose everything he had and his life because of his allegiance to the Living God.

Thirdly, Daniel loved his people with all his heart. This is shown by his willingness to speak well of his friends and seek wisdom to solve a mystery from the king; as a result, the lives of wise men in Babylon were preserved. Daniel fasted and prayed for the restoration of Jerusalem and forgiveness for the sins of the Israelites. The beginning of great things in the life of a leader starts with learning to love people in the private chamber of their thoughts. Their attitude toward their fellow people must be of love and service.

Fourthly, Daniel committed himself to learn and develop his mind. Daniel understood that a well-trained mind is an asset in the life of a leader. One scholar of leadership comments on Daniel and his colleagues' attitude toward learning:

They placed themselves where God could bless them. They avoided that which would weaken their powers and improved every opportunity to become intelligent in all lines of learning. They followed the rules of life that could not fail to give them strength of intellect. They sought to gain knowledge for one purpose that they might honor God.[51]

Success results from a determination to use every opportunity to develop your mind. Daniel never wavered on this principle. As you ascend to a position of power and authority, the tasking of your mind increases; if you are well-trained, the investment will pay abundantly.

Some suggestions when choosing your personal values

As insight we gain from the life of Daniel: he chose his values based on the love of his God and the character of his God. The character of God is the 10 commandments, observed from one generation to the next. When you choose your personal values to guide your life, they should be anchored on the eternal moral laws of God—you will never go wrong.

When choosing personal values to guide you, they must be based on the desire to develop your abilities and talents. Cultivate your health to be the best of the best, and to be the best human being you can be, who reflects the image and likeness of God.

When choosing your personal values, they must be based on love for your fellow men and on the desire to give the best service to your family, church, organization, country and world. Your values should be based on the desire to and premise of serving others with an open heart. Always, ask how you can offer the best service to your friends, without waiting for them to serve you. Always, ask how you can make them smile, instead of asking what they can do for you to smile.

THE PROACTIVE MIND

Daniel exhibited the power of a proactive mind when he was presented with foods that were offered to idols in the school of leadership in Babylon. This is how Daniel spoke to the master assigned over him, Hananiah, Mishael and Azari:

Please test your servants for ten days: Give us nothing but vegetables to eat and water to drink. Then compare our appearance with that of the young men who eat the royal food and treat your servants under what you see. So, he agreed to this and tested them for ten days. At the end of the ten

days, they looked healthier and better nourished
than any of the young men who ate the royal food.[52]

Daniel did not just refuse to eat the king's food because it was unclean, he also provided alternative food to nourish their bodies. He did not end there to assure their supervisor; he proposed a 10-day trial of their health. If they were well-nourished, then they should be left to continue with their eating habits. If not, they would eat the king's portion.

Proactive individuals take responsibility for their actions and habits; they take initiative and keep their commitments.

Proactive individuals accept responsibility when they realize that they have made a mistake. They design and take actions that help them correct the mistake. They plan and take steps that help them develop behavior that will enhance their future and well-being. They plan their actions based on the values they have developed and established.

Instead of being reactive to what has happened that they do not have control of, they take action that is based on their belief system and values. They base their happiness on the eternal strength of spiritual muscles, instead of depending on social profiling or people's opinions. But as proactive individuals realize they have no control over the choices and actions they take, they also realize that they do not have control of the results, because the results are determined by the natural laws and God.

Proactive individuals take initiative. According to Stephen Covey, taking initiative means, "recognizing our responsibility to make things happen."[53] Instead of waiting for people to decide for them, leaders take the first initiative to make things happen to match their goals and values.

When Daniel was offered foods that were not healthy and spiritually-nourishing, as instructed in the Word of God, with wisdom he requested of his instructor to be given alternative food, food from plants and water instead. When the instructor was reluctant, Daniel suggested he be tested for 10 days to see if his health was better than the rest of the young people; if his health was better after the 10 days, the officer may decide according to his wisdom.

Finally, proactive individuals respect and keep their commitments to their friends and followers. Proactive individuals keep their end goal in mind. The main goal of a leader is to be of service to his fellow men, to be a blessing and develop lasting trust with their followers—they always keep their commitments. They avoid making promises that they cannot keep. Their commitments are few and well-chosen to make sure they're all kept:

Behavioral integrity is linked to the concept of trust...If someone typically does not keep their

*promises, those around them will see that person as
less trustworthy. As a result, such a person might
have to offer more explanations to maintain trust.
People who keep their word and follow through
on actions would not need to explain themselves
as much. The presence or absence of these explanations could offer a clue to whether a CEO's actions
and words were congruent.*[54]

Leaders connect with fellow leaders and followers
on a personal level. This can only be accomplished
by developing trust, and trust can only be achieved
by keeping promises and commitments. If you always
promise people things that you cannot fulfill, your
reputation will stink, and you will lose your trusted
friends. Fulfilled commitments confirm your loyalty to
your people. Fulfilled commitments cement your inner
purity of thoughts and love for others. Proactive people
keep their responsibilities as leaders in their hearts.

Proactive leaders in the Bible

In the book of 2 Samuel, chapter 11, the prophet
Nathaniel visited King David. During their conversation, the prophet narrated a story that pointed to
the sin of David against God and Uriah. The moment
David realized his mistake, he did not shy away or deny
his sins; he humbled himself, took full responsibility
for his mistakes and sought forgiveness from God. He

endured the consequences of his sins with grace. The full confession of the prayer of David is in Psalm 51.

Many leaders fall short in this way; some never want to take responsibility for their actions—they like to blame others when things go wrong. The beginning of transformation in your life is taking full responsibility for your life and your mistakes.

Another story that has inspired people for ages is the story of Goliath and David. No wonder David was the revered leader! When the Philistines showed up to fight Israel, they came with a tactic that stunned the army of Israel and their king. The Philistines introduced a giant named Goliath, who challenged the children of Israel to bring a mighty man to fight against him; if the Israelite won, the Philistines would be their slaves, and if the Israelite lost, they would be the slaves of the Philistines.

This proclamation created panic and fear in the Israelites, and they were all losing hope. In the entire army, there was no one courageous enough to fight Goliath; no one devised a solution. The proactive mind of shepherd David saved the entire nation from demise and shame. David's proactive spirit was based on the promises of God. Through his courage and faith in God, he won against the Philistine. If you want to be a proactive individual, why not fill your brain with the promises of God? With faith, you can move mountains.

The story of Zacchaeus is a testimony that proactive individuals do not allow themselves to be taken hostage by their shortcomings and limitations. They create ways to compensate for their limitations. He wanted to see Jesus, but because of the multitude, it was impossible to see Jesus due to his shortness. So, he thought to himself, "I will climb a tree," though he was one of the richest men in Israel, so that when Jesus passed by, Zacchaeus would see him. His creativity paid off; he climbed a tree, and when Jesus passed by, he recognized the sincerity of Zacchaeus's heart. He looked up and said, "Today, salvation has come to your house." The man was rewarded because of his proactive mind. There are no limits or problems that cannot be overcome—it depends on the state of your own mind.

Ruth and Naomi are another powerful story to show the power of keeping your commitments to your partners. Naomi and her husband fled famine in Israel and went to the land of the Moabites. While they were there, their two sons married wives from the Moabites. Unfortunately, Naomi's husband and two sons died. They left her with her two daughters-in-law. She told them, "I'm about to go back to my native country, so please go back to your mothers' houses, and there you may find men to marry you and raise your own family."

But Ruth said, "I will never leave, your God will be my God, your burial place is that where I will be buried." Naomi insisted that Ruth should go back to her household, but Ruth refused and followed Naomi. She kept her promises when they arrived in Israel. They kept working together, helping each other, until

God blessed Ruth with a husband and a son. Through the line of Ruth, David and Jesus were born. This happened because Ruth was proactive enough to keep her commitment to her mother-in-law.

THE POWER OF PRAYER IN THE LIFE OF A LEADER

The habit of praying daily is the source of wisdom, knowledge and strength to a leader; prayer is a necessity for the successful functioning of a leader. Prayers connect the leader to God, who reveals wisdom and knowledge to the leader as he tries to solve problems and plan for a better future.

For the leader to have vitality and strength to do his job efficiently, he needs support from Heaven. To endure disappointment and hardship, prayers are very important and the main source of strength and courage.

Now when Daniel knew that the writing was signed, he went home. And in his upper room, with his windows open toward Jerusalem, he knelt down on his knees three times that day, and prayed and gave thanks before his God, as was his custom [habits] since early days.[55]

Then Daniel returned to his house and explained the matter to his friends Hananiah, Mishael and Azariah. He urged them to plead for mercy from the God of heaven concerning this mystery, so he

and his friends might not be executed with the rest
of the wise men of Babylon. During the night God
revealed the mystery to Daniel in a vision.[56]

Then I set my face toward the Lord God to make a
request by prayer and supplications, with fasting,
sackcloth, and ashes.[57]

Firstly, Daniel cultivated a habit of praying three times a day; in the morning, in the afternoon, in the evening. These were well-selected hours of the day for him to connect with God. These were times he dedicated in giving praise and thanksgiving to the King of kings and the Creator of everything. In these hours, he would focus his mind to learn, relax and reflect on the mercies and mighty work of God.

Before sin entered this world, God used to visit Adam and Eve in the garden during evening. These hours were set apart to fellowship with God, to unite with and learn from him. The Father visited his children every evening to know their well-being. They shared with God their discoveries while exploring the garden and the happiness of their friendship; from these times, they gained divine insight from God of life and comfort. There is great warmth and joy in communion with God.

God is the Creator of the world, the universe and all that is in it, and we owe our lives to Him. He desires to cultivate a personal relationship with each one of us. Most of us think prayer must be very complicated and complex, but the Lord desires to develop a deep and intimate relationship with us through simple activities in prayer that every individual can do.

For example, having a cup of tea in a private room to sit in the presence of the Lord, just you and God relaxing, sharing his love and grace together. Wait for the Lord to speak with you for a few minutes. Each idea that He inspires, write it down without pondering if it will work or not; your goal is to listen to the Creator while He speaks to you. Later, take a tour of the ideas God inspired in you. It will surprise you how powerful you can be. This process is very healthy to your brain and heart as well. It gives the heart the tranquility it needs to process and balance all the emotional stimuli that fires every minute to your center of spirituality.

The key thing is that Daniel developed the habit of prayer. God is the source of strength, knowledge and wisdom, and anyone who is open to receive and accept His gifts will get them during prayer. Leaders cultivate a habit of connecting with God. Moses spent most of his time communing with God; through these lessons, God revealed His wisdom and plans to Moses.

Jesus used to wake up very early in the morning to pray. During these quiet moments, Jesus united with his Father. In these sacred hours, Jesus fellowshipped with his Father in a song of praise, giving thanks for the work that his Father enabled him to do. In these moments, Jesus shared with his Father his pains, his disappointments, his plans, and presented to his Father the needs of his friends. By doing so, he found relief and peace. God is very interested in developing a friendship with you in everything you do. In the quietness of communion with God, you will find peace and tranquility of heart and mind. You will find strength to affirm your purpose and commitment to God and friends.

Secondly, Daniel sought wisdom and understanding from God through prayer. We see Daniel seeking God in prayer to gain wisdom and understanding of problems, as they were presented to him. After King Nebuchadnezzar presented the problem that needed to be solved, and there were none to solve the mystery of his dream, Daniel sought the solution in prayer from God. There are many problems today that human intelligence cannot solve—only the Divine can solve them.

Daniel encouraged his friends to unite in prayer to seek wisdom and knowledge from God. God rewarded them by answering their request. As an answer to their prayer, God revealed the truth that troubled the king to Daniel. God revealed the dream and its interpretation to Daniel in a vision at night. God has ordained prayer to be the means by which mankind can unite with Him to gain knowledge, wisdom and power. So, before you run to solve a problem, run first and pray to the Living God; ask for His wisdom on how to solve the problem that is troubling you.

Through prayer, Abraham received the promise of a son in whom the assurance of being the father of many nations would be fulfilled. It was during prayer that God appeared to Abraham in a dream and showed him the vision of the people of God and assured of the fulfillment of His promises. The vision of a coming messiah was revealed to Abraham through prayer.

Joshua, after the defeat of Israel's army by the little city of Ai, humbled himself in prayer to seek the reason of defeat. The Lord revealed to him the cause of defeat, that the children of Israel had committed sins. Through prayer, the Lord opened the eyes of his general.

We admire the wisdom and depth of King Solomon insights; we normally forget that the endowment of these gifts was bestowed to him through prayer. After Solomon took the leadership of the nation of Israel, the Lord appeared unto Him and spoke to him in a dream. "Ask anything you want Me to do for you," and Solomon requested wisdom, knowledge and a discerning heart so he may lead the nation of Israel to prosperity and peace.

In the book of Daniel, chapters 7-11, we read that Daniel was visited by the angel Gabriel, and he revealed to Daniel the meaning of the dreams and succession of kingdoms until the end of this world. It became normal for heavenly beings to visit Daniel, and it is a lesson to leaders that the Living God will send His angels to give wisdom and knowledge to His servants during prayer.

It was in prayer on a mountain that Jesus united with Elijah and Moses in a sweet conversation. Jesus did not tell us what they discussed in that meeting, but on this occasion, Jesus found strength and comfort from these holy men.

It's in these times of quiet that angels visit the servants of God to strengthen them and reveal to them the power and wisdom of God. In these special moments, the leader receives new ideas for business, life improvement, spiritual development and visions. Wise leaders keep a note and a pen, and whenever the Lord reveals good ideas, they write down all the beautiful ideas as they flow into their brain from God.

Lastly, Daniel sought mercies, reconciliation and strength through prayer in chapter 9 of the book of Daniel. During this time, Daniel offered prayer for the children of Israel who were in Babylon, because they disobeyed the laws of God. Many of them died during the destruction of the city and temple in Jerusalem. It was a shame to the nation of Israel, which was considered the light of the world because they worshiped the Mighty King of the universe.

After, Daniel learned that the time for exile was nearing (70 years). He devoted his energy in prayer to seek God's forgiveness and the restoration of the nation of Israel. God sent His angel, who shed light on the plan to restore the nation of Israel to its former glory. The leader is an intercessor; his work is to reconcile people with God, facilitate a reconciliation and seek the healing of the land. So, the leader stands between

God and His people—between death and life, between shame and glory.

Moses is an example of a leader who devoted his life to intercede for the people. The children of Israel were rebellious at heart. In one occasion, Moses went to the mount to pray, and he stayed there for 40 days. When Moses was delayed coming down from the mountain, the host of Israel went to Aaron and pressed him hard to make them an idol.

Aaron formed an image of gold, and the people worshiped and praised it. While Moses was on the mountain, God said to him, "Your people have gone astray." When Moses arrived at the foot of the mountain and saw what was going on, he was enraged. He commanded those who did not bow to the idol to kill the rebellious. After, he told the people to keep praying, because he was going on the mountain to intercede for them—perhaps God would forgive their sins.

Through his earnest prayer, the sins of Israel were atoned. Moses was the bridge that connected the people with God. He carried their sins on his shoulders and made them his own. Through selfless commitment to serve the Israelites, they were preserved from the wrath of God.

Leaders are intercessors for their people, no matter how rebellious they are. The moment you lead people, you become their father: you protect them, bless them, forgive them and seek forgiveness for them. To fulfill this role, you must unite with God so that your actions and words becomes springs of life to your followers. Prayer is a powerhouse for the leader to gain wisdom, understanding and mercies from God.

THE POWER OF MUTUAL FRIENDSHIP

A leader enriches and nurtures friendship with a group of people who think and act in a spirit of harmony. These are not the same as people who you celebrate parties with or friends at church or work. These are people who you select wisely to be in your inner circle. Adhering to Solomon's wisdom, "The righteous choose their friends carefully."[58] Normally, the group comprises three to four people. To these mutual friends, you go for encouragement, edifying and bonding for the purpose of coming to the union of mind in doing and creating great things in life.

When Daniel faced a problem, he opted for the high ground: "Then Daniel returned to his house and explained the matter to his friends Hananiah, Mishael and Azari. He urged them to plead [pray] for mercy from the God of heaven concerning this mystery, so he and his friends might not be executed with the rest of the wise men of Babylon."[59] To solve the mystery dream, Daniel did not go to strangers to find solutions, though it may work sometimes, but he consulted his inner circle partners for wisdom and understanding from God. When two or more individuals come before God in the spirit of love to seek wisdom, Heaven will never shut its doors.

Let us imagine this scenario: if your destination is to go North, and you are spending time with the people heading South, eventually, you will adopt their ways and techniques to navigate routes to the South, and you will be transformed to think and act like them. As you fellowship with them, you will be influenced without even realizing; as a result, you join the caravan to the South. In a twinkling of an eye, you are in the South, wondering how in the world you got there, because if you go to the place where you were not meant to be planted, you will be frustrated and confused. If you are not spared, you will perish in the foreign land.

The danger is that it is hard to go back to where you belong, the true destination of yours, because now the journey to go back has doubled and your mindset has shifted. The people who would have made your journey to the North easier are not with you; at the moment, they are celebrating the achievement of their hard work and commitment.

Then you will say, "I know this is the place I was meant to be, and I will stay here." But you were destined to fly like an eagle and see the glory of high ground, you are now stuck with tortoises who do not know what it's like to fly; what they have known since their inception is to crawl.

How tragic. Most of us miss the blessings that the Lord has set for us to achieve and conquer, the freedom that has been designed for us to enjoy in the free sky. The main reason for this is that we spend time with the wrong people, those who do not understand and are not interested in our destination. We end up frustrated and disappointed, wondering, "Why?"

To apply the meaning, let's consider King Solomon's wisdom: "Do not make friends with a hot-tempered person, do not associate with one angered, or you may learn their ways and get yourself ensnared."[60] The principle behind this passage is that the associations you nurture in your life will mold your influence and character.

Daniel, the man of God who knew the power of this principle, spent most of his time with men who shared the same values, mission and vision that he cherished: "As iron sharpens iron, so one person sharpens another."[61] These are the men he shared his burdens with and prayed together with; these were men filled with the Holy Spirit.

Hananiah, Mishael and Azariah, the inner circle friends of Daniel, shared the same values he did. They worshiped the same God, ate the same food and had the same level of integrity. Their minds were married to each other's thinking and doing. When Daniel faced a hard problem to solve like the one in Daniel chapter 2, he shared with his friends to seek mercies and wisdom from God to solve it.

Powerful leaders form mutual friendships, applying the heaven-born principle: "Walk with the wise and become wise."[62]

The inner circle of Moses was comprised of Joshua and Aron. Later, the 70 elders joined Moses on the leadership team. Joshua and Aron were the right hands of Moses.

The inner circle of Joshua was comprised of Caleb; these two men shared the same faith and courage amid difficulties.

The inner circle of Elijah was comprised of Elisha, whom the Lord appointed to be trained under the leadership of Elijah to take the position of prophet after the departure of Elijah.

The inner circle of Jesus was comprised of Peter, James and John. These are men whom Jesus showed his glory and took for prayer when things were tough. The Lord values and cherishes the benefits of mutual friendship. These men became a force of power after the ascension of Jesus; they encouraged their fellow brothers to keep the light burning in the world.

The inner circle of Paul was comprised of Silas, Luke and Timothy. Luke wrote a lot about the ministry of Paul; the message has been an anchor and blessing to the world. Silas joined Paul in preaching the Gospel to the world. Because of the nature of Paul's mission, he had several mutual friends to support him in his ministry. I think Luke was the most prominent of all.

I think it's wise for people joined in a partnership of marriage to make each other a best friend; nurture your relationship so you inspire one another to achieve great things. How powerful will you be if you think with a unity of mind and heart?

Having this kind of friendship is good for your health, manages stress, shares burdens, builds each other up and appreciates each other; it serves as the powerhouse to generate ideas and momentum to start actions. When two or three come in harmony of heart to seek God's wisdom, the Lord is present to support them. Our heavenly Father enjoys blessing the union when two or three people work together in the spirit of mutual friendship:

> *Two are better than one, because they have a good return for their labor: If either of them falls down, one can help the other up but pity anyone who falls and has no one to help them up. Also, if two lie down together, they will keep warm. But how can one keep warm alone? Though one may be overpowered, two can defend themselves. A cord of three strands is not quickly broken.*[63]

Napoleon Hill emphasized this point: "Men take on the nature and the habits and the power of thought of those with whom they associate in a spirit of sympathy and harmony."[64] I think this statement is worth great attention for leaders.

SEEKING UNDERSTANDING

A leader must possess a burning desire to understand the depth of a problem or subject presented before them;

they must desire to understand the people around them and those they are trying to influence to follow them. Without understanding, the leader is blind, and their own inclination will deceive and mislead them and those around them. Daniel nurtured the spirit of desiring to understand whatever subject before him:

I, Daniel, was troubled in spirit, and the visions that passed through my mind disturbed me. I approached one of those standing there and asked him the meaning of all this. So, he told me and gave me the interpretation of these things.[65]

Then I wanted to know the meaning of the fourth beast which was different from all the others and most terrifying, with its iron teeth and bronze claws \the beast that crushed and devoured its victims and trampled underfoot whatever was left. I also wanted to know about the ten horns on its head and about the other horn that came up, before which three of them fell the horn that looked more imposing than the others and that had eyes and a mouth that spoke boastfully.[66]

In the first year of Darius son of Xerxes (a Mede by descent), who was made ruler over the Babylonian kingdom in the first year of his reign, I, Daniel, understood from the Scriptures, according to the word of the Lord given to Jeremiah the prophet,

that the desolation of Jerusalem would last seventy
years. So, I turned to the Lord God and pleaded
with him in prayer and petition, in fasting, and in
sackcloth and ashes.[67]

While I was still in prayer, Gabriel, the man I
had seen in the earlier vision, came to me in swift
flight about the time of the evening sacrifice. He
instructed me and said to me, Daniel; I have now
come to give your insight and understanding. As
soon as you began to pray, a word went out, which
I have come to tell you, for you are highly esteemed.
Therefore, consider the word and understand the
vision.[68]

In chapter 7 of the book of Daniel, the Lord revealed great visions to Daniel, which he could not comprehend; so, Daniel approached an angel of God and requested the meaning of the vision. God rewarded Daniel with the interpretation of the vision. Every time that Daniel could not comprehend the meaning of a vision, he requested the interpretation of it. Again, and again, God rewarded Daniel with the meaning of them.

In chapter 10, Daniel fasted for about three weeks, seeking to understand the meaning of the visions, which God presented to him in chapters 7-9. The Lord sent His angel Gabriel to reveal the meaning of dreams and visions.

In chapter 9, Daniel sought understanding in the books of the prophet Jeremiah and the Torah. Through reading and research, Daniel understood the prophecy of Jeremiah concerning the nation of Israel, that it was God who sent them into exile for 70 years because of their transgressions against God's laws. In response to this understanding, Daniel set himself to seek forgiveness and strength for his people from God.

Daniel desired to understand and gain the meaning of problems as he faced them. This habit gave him tremendous power and insight into the future; this is a key habit for a successful leader. Daniel knew very well that if he understood a problem deeply and broadly, he had solved half of it. Some problems need only to be understood to solve them.

To understand a problem, you must adjust your thinking to adapt to the new challenges or reality. This may involve adjusting your binoculars to zoom either out or in to see the challenge distinctly, or it may involve isolating your thoughts for a moment to allow yourself to see the problem without the bias of your own perceptions and judgments. I will discuss techniques and tools to understand various problems in the upcoming chapter on solving difficult problems. In this chapter, we will focus more on techniques that will help you understand other people.

The leader must nourish the attitude of seeking to understand first, before opening their mouth or acting. This is vital because if the leader misunderstands their followers or colleagues, they multiply the problem instead of solving it and bring disaster to themselves and the entire organization.

Habits that hinder leaders from understanding their followers:

1. Pride/arrogance: Leaders who think they know all will fail in understanding other people.
2. Health problems: a problem with your hearing abilities can prevent you from understanding your followers. As a leader, you must make sure you take care of your body, because it is the means of receiving information.
3. Fatigue: if you are tired, you will not pay attention to detail. Fatigue reduces the strength to concentrate on small details.
4. Conditions of the surrounding environment: this includes noise, bad smells, rubbish and all that can stand between you and your ability to pay attention.
5. The picture we hold about ourselves, the world and the surrounding people.
6. Lack of understanding our strengths and weaknesses: knowledge of yourself will help you understand your fellow leaders and followers.

How can we understand other individuals endowed by the Creator with their own ability to choose and to act independently? Here are a few tips on developing your skills to understand people:

Firstly, desire to understand. This is the starting point for every great endeavor in life. You can never replace burning desire with anything else. If you do not desire to understand others, there is no motivation to search out those tools that will help you enter the world of other individuals. To understand others, you must walk in their shoes and experience the world as they experience it; this requires tremendous sacrifice, energy and commitment.

Secondly, put your paradigm aside. A paradigm is the picture you hold about yourself, the surrounding people and the world around you; entering the other person's paradigm requires shifting your eyes from yourself to the other person—how they grew up, what kinds of words were spoken to them, what friends they have around them, the language they speak, what kind of books they read, what kind of pain they endured during childhood. These elements shape how people perceive the world around them.

Entering someone else's world is like being exported to a foreign city or country. You need to learn their language, cuisine, traditions—their way of life. With this perspective, any moment you meet someone in the marketplace, office, school, church, gym, it is wise to consider them as a foreign country that needs to be explored. The marks that makes someone unique from you must be considered and handled with great care and skill. These marks are sealed with fire, engraved on our nerves, and they influence how we react and respond to another person's stimulus.

These emotions are electrical imprints that have burned on our nerves and leave a great memory that creates a powerful image of who we are and how we view ourselves and others. They can be a great source of strength to achieve great things in life or a great mountain to prevent us from reaching our full development and enjoyment of blessing given to us by our Creator.

These scars can prevent us from enjoying a bountiful relationship with others; every time we try to make a move, they pull us back. Unfortunately, we cast these pains and disappointment on others, and they prevent us from understanding our friends, partners, relatives and coworkers.

The great advantage we have as human beings is the ability to choose and adopt new ways to change and transform ourselves to a greater height of enjoyment of friendships.

A leader must understand what prevents him from understanding others, so he can correct those mistakes. The leader must understand these scars and understand why people act the way they do and why they behave in certain ways, to understand them deeply. To enter other people's inner world requires total immersion in the other person's feelings and thinking. The wisest leader will gain skills to enter this inner world; leaders must touch and see the invisible world of their followers to learn what makes them act as they do.

Thirdly, learn to focus with your whole heart, mind and body; we call this total presence. It's difficult to pay attention while you're distracted by other activities. The reasons that most of us do not enjoy or comprehend the very things we are doing now is that we are divided in our heart; we are juggling too many things at once. Leaders know the wisdom of immersing oneself in the world of other people to understand them and absorb every bit of information shared with them. When you have a clear picture of what they said, it gives you a crystal-clear perspective of the needs of the other person.

This means that you put aside all the thoughts and preconceived ideas you hold about others. The problem that faces most of us is that even before we have listened to the story of the other person, we have made an opinion about them. This places a black veil between us, and our attention gets divided, because we do not see the need to listen to others with full concentration. As a result, misunderstanding and confusion dominates.

We must remember that people are selfish by nature; my needs come first before yours. If you devote your time to listen to the other person, it is eye-opening. Leaders seek to understand first before being understood; because they know when they understand their followers' needs, it's easy to touch their hearts.

Fourthly, put the needs of the other person first. That means, for the moment, you sacrifice your needs, so you can see the needs of the other person distinctly. If you think in simple terms, if you're going forward, you must focus your eyes and attention on the road ahead of you; if you look sideways while walking forward, you will trip. The same principle applies to your inner eyes; you must detach your needs and pay full attention to what the other person is communicating with you. Then you can see the full picture of what your friend is seeing or feeling about themselves. The reason for doing this is to build trust, so that later, your needs may be met by your followers.

In chapter 10, Daniel records that he avoided good food and choice meat, no lotion touched his skin for three weeks, he mourned and sought understanding from God. We see Daniel sacrifice his own needs to focus on the needs of God. Trying to understand what kind of message the Lord was telling him, he concentrated his energy, spiritual faculties and physical faculties to understand the message of God. The Lord rewarded him by sending His angel to explain and give understanding to Daniel concerning the vision and dreams.

Now, here is the secret repeated to us again and again: a person of God places their desire to understand God's message above their own needs; this is a trumpet sounding! We should deny ourselves the very things we cherish in seeking to understand God. The same principle applies to each one of us—we must sacrifice our needs in seeking to understanding from our fellow men.

This means you must put aside that phone distracting you, the wine that is preventing you from understanding your partner, the love of money, power, or a position that is depriving you the privilege to understanding your fellow men. The call is to humble yourself, go to your friends and pay attention to what they are trying to tell you. By doing so, you will understand them, and they will understand you.

This principle requires integrity of heart; if your heart is not clean and honest, it will never allow you to sit down and pay attention to your fellow people. When your heart is clean and genuine, it will push you to listen to your friends. Most people are afraid, because they know if they sit down to listen, their shortcomings will be put to light—that will challenge their ego. Integrity comes because you have learned to accept your shortcomings and work toward improving them; because of that, you will do the same to your fellow men, so they can feel comfortable to seek the same relief by letting go of their shortcomings.

Fifthly, understand your needs and wants distinctly; this will help you see how other people desire to be understood as you are. Having a total understanding of yourself with a clear picture and knowing how your own brain works will open a door to appreciate other people around you. The very things we want for ourselves are the same things others desire but expressed in different ways, according to the paradigm of the other person's lenses.

Sixthly, seek insight through reading literature. Reading has been proven to be a powerful source of wisdom to understand people's behavior. The problems you are facing today, someone has experienced before and written about it. Searching for information through literature will open your eyes to heights that you never thought existed. Reading is the most powerful tool ever given to mankind, because those who know how to read and learn to apply the knowledge, they have gained will conquer any problem in this life. Even if you do not find a clear-cut solution to your problem, someone will give you insight to design the solution that fits the needs of your situation

Seventhly, seek wisdom to understand others through prayer. The Lord will never leave you blind. After we have done all we can to sympathize with others, but things are not clear to us, then we can turn to prayer to seek God, so He can reveal what we are missing. Sometimes, we do not understand others because we are blinded by our own ignorance. When we seek God in prayer, He opens our minds so we can see our need of Him and His Word.

Lastly, visualizing paying attention to the other person for the sake of understanding. This is a powerful form of creative thinking. When you make a mental picture of yourself, you commit to action that helps to achieve your goal, motivating your brain to focus and propelling you to take more action. Your action first starts as thoughts and then translates into actions, so if your thoughts are correct and are channeled toward a specific goal, you will achieve it. Visualizing that you are using all the gifts God has endowed you to understanding others will pay a hundredfold.

The benefits of understanding people

Understanding helps the leader execute justice to the right people. Refer to the story of Solomon and the two prostitutes in 1 Kings chapter 3.

Understanding helps to connect with people easier. The goal of a leader is to inspire people to think big, understand their problems and design better solutions to live better and happier. This can only be accomplished by connecting with people emotionally, intellectually and spiritually.

Understanding gives wisdom to the leader to answer correctly and prompt their audience. Most leaders fail in this sphere of human connection. If someone is hungry and you are trying to teach him new ideas, they will resent you and disown your good intention. The problem is that you did not understand their needs. To speak to the hearts and minds of people, you must understand their hidden needs. Words spoken to the right person in the right circumstance with the correct intensity bring healing and joy.

Deep understanding helps in resolving relational problems. Many problems will be solved if the parties sit down and talk face-to-face, heart-to-heart.

Understanding preserves the leader. Leaders with foresight will avoid myriad difficulties in leading their fellow people.

Understanding helps people store wealth. People of great understanding will store for themselves and others the blessings this world has to offer.

Be sure you know the condition of your flocks, give careful attention to your herds for riches do not endure forever, and a crown is not secure for all generations. When the hay is removed and new growth appears and the grass from the hills is gathered in, the lambs will provide you with clothing, and the goats with the price of a field. You will have plenty of goat's milk to feed your family and to nourish your female servants.[69]

Understanding will honor the leader with power and strength. Knowledge is power. Knowing how to use knowledge to inspire people will give you tremendous strength to accomplish great things.

FILLED WITH THE SPIRIT OF GOD (THE HOLY SPIRIT)

When a person is overshadowed by the Spirit of the Living God; God endows that person with wisdom, understanding, and skills to do excellent work. Excellent work results from hard work and the fruit of the spirit that controls the heart of the leader. One author affirmed this truth in his writings: "It is through the Holy Spirit that every good work is accomplished."[70] Among the fruits of the Holy Spirit are beauty, creativity and excellence in working. Leaders are to be known by their followers because of their purity of thoughts which manifest in actions.

Because Daniel was full of the Spirit of God, King Nebuchadnezzar requested Daniel interpret the dream he had in the night concerning a big tree that reached to Heaven. This is what the king spoke to Daniel: "Belteshazzar, chief of the magicians, because I know that the Spirit of the Holy God is in you, and no secret troubles you, explain to me the visions of my dream I have seen, and its interpretation."[71] The king desired to understand the dream, but there was no one in his kingdom to interpret except Daniel, the man of God. Daniel revealed the meaning of the dream. The Spirit of God had given Daniel understanding to solve the mystery.

On another occasion, the grandson of Nebuchadnezzar, while enjoying and celebrating with his concubines, saw strange handwriting on the wall, and he was scared to death. He thought to find the meaning of the inscription, but none could solve the riddle among the wise men. The news reached the queen, who was acquainted with Daniel, and she recommended to the king:

*There is a man in your kingdom in whom is the
Spirit of the Holy God. And in the days of your
father, light and understanding and wisdom, like
the wisdom of the gods, were found in him; Because
an excellent spirit, knowledge, understanding,
interpreting dreams, solving riddles, and explaining
enigmas were found in this Daniel, whom the king
named Belteshazzar.*[72]

After Daniel was brought before the king, this is
how the king responded: "The king spoke, and said to
Daniel, are you that Daniel who is one of the captives
from Judah, whom my father the king brought from
Judah? I have heard of you, that the Spirit of God is
in you, and that light and understanding and excellent
wisdom are found in you."[73] The Spirit of God made
Daniel greater than any genius that ever lived. The
Spirit of God impacts knowledge and wisdom to solve
hard problems.

In Daniel chapter 6, Daniel was found to be an
excellent worker among the three administrators in
the whole kingdom of Babylon because the Spirit of the
Living God occupied his mind. This is what the scroll
of Daniel records: "Then this Daniel was preferred
above the presidents and princes, because an excellent
spirit was in him; and the king thought to set him over
the whole realm."[74] When a leader is controlled by the
Spirit of the Living God, he does not do mediocre jobs;
he performs extraordinary work. King Darius thought

to place Daniel as a head over the whole kingdom. This how the Spirit of the Living God expressed Himself in the leadership of Daniel.

The Spirit of God has expressed Himself in many lives of great leaders in the Bible, as powerful movers and doers

Joseph interpreted the dreams of Pharaoh because the Holy Spirit filled him and led the nation of Egypt through a severe famine. When Pharaoh heard the wisdom of Joseph in interpreting the dream and the counsel on how to prepare for the famine, he was astonished, and proclaimed, "There is no other wise person in the kingdom compared to Joseph because of the Spirit of God in him." There are problems that cannot be solved by using human ingenuity—they require divine wisdom.

Through the power of the Holy Spirit, Moses led the children of Israel through the desert for 40 years. Dealing with rebellious people and an untrained host of men is difficult. The wisdom and strength of Moses was because of the power of the Holy Spirit that controlled him. The Holy Spirit made his mind understand the divine precepts and the will of God. God told Moses to commission 70 elders to help in leading the people, and God took some measure of his Spirit's power and filled the elders so that they may lead to support Moses.

Joshua, through the power of the Holy Spirit, conquered Jericho and led the children of Israel to inherit the Promised Land of Canaan. After Moses laid his hands-on Joshua, Joshua was filled with the Holy Spirit. The Spirit of God counseled him in leading the Israelites to the Promised Land. The Spirit inspired Joshua to conquer the enemies of God's people.

The mighty Spirit of God controlled Samson, and he fought a one-person war against the entire nation of Philistine. The inspired life of Samson as the judge of Israel proves and demonstrates what a person who is controlled by the living Spirit of God can accomplish. The Spirit of God made Samson a formidable warrior, who knew not fear against a multitude of enemy soldiers.

Both David and Solomon proved to be powerful leaders because of the power of the Holy Spirit that overshadowed them. The glorious leadership of David in Israel was accomplished through the anointment of the Divine Spirit. David knew how to associate and work with soldiers due to the wisdom of the Holy Spirit. The same conduit manifested in the life and leadership of his son Solomon. The entire world of his time desired to hear and learn from his wise tongue.

Elijah and Elisha could perceive the thoughts of their enemies because the Spirit of the Living God revealed it to them. These two prophets were the eyes and ears of Israel. They could reveal the thoughts of commanders of the enemies of the nation of Israel. The Holy Spirit searched the hearts of men to know their true motives. When the leader is filled with Holy Spirit, the Spirit of God will reveal hidden thoughts of people for the carrying out of God's purpose.

Jesus was born through the power of the Holy Spirit, through a woman who was a virgin. There is no limit when an individual is overshadowed by the Holy Spirit.

The mighty work performed by the Son of God was done through the leading of the Holy Spirit. After the baptism of Jesus by John the Baptist, the Spirit of God descended on Jesus in the form of a dove—that was the beginning of the great work of Jesus Christ. He raised the dead, healed the sick, cast out demons and brought spiritual healing to many people. Words of life and grace by the Son of God were living bread of life, through the power of the Holy Spirit.

Who is the Holy Spirit?

The Holy Scriptures present the Holy Spirit as the third being in the Trinity. Jesus said, "When you baptize people, do it in the name of the Father, the Son and the Holy Spirit." When Jesus addressed his disciples concerning the Holy Spirit, he referred to Him as "He." That means He is the intelligent, omniscient, omnipotent and omnipresent God. The Spirit of God was present in the beginning of creation. The prophet Ezekiel saw in a vision the throne of God and the living beings in Heaven following the leading of the Holy Spirit, wherever He goes.

The Spirit of God is not a mere force that you can control as you wish, as many people think, but the

Spirit of God is beyond our limited understanding. You cannot control Him; He is the one who controls you. The temple of the Holy Spirit is your body; He dwells in your heart. The Spirit of God makes everything in the universe work according to the divine purpose of God.

The nature of the Holy Spirit is a mystery that God has not revealed to mankind, so trying to explain what He looks like is a futile endeavor. The Spirit of God reveals Himself through the Holy Scriptures and through ordained works of God.

More roles of the Holy Spirit in the life of a leader

The Holy Spirit is counselor. According to the promise of Jesus Christ in John chapter 14, the Holy Spirit will give heartfelt counsel to a leader, to make the right decision that will enhance the lives of their followers.

The Holy Spirit gives an understanding and discerning heart to the leader. Refer to the story of Apostle Peter in Acts 5, as well as the story of King Solomon and two prostitutes in 1 Kings 3. God gifted Daniel with an understanding and discerning heart to solve difficult problems as they presented to him.

The Holy Spirit can manifest Himself through mighty work, as in the lives of Jesus, Samson, Moses, Elisha and the apostles. Miracles will accompany leaders filled with the Holy Spirit.

The Holy Spirit sharpens the technical skills of the leader. In Exodus 31:1-3, we see that the Lord fills His leader with the Holy Spirit to accomplish technical works in building God's tabernacle.

The Holy Spirit fills the leader with wisdom to make hard decisions. If a leader desires to make decisions that will bless his people, it will benefit him to surrender to the leading of the Holy Spirit.

The Holy Spirit gives endurance to the leader as he or she deals with difficult situations. The leader thrives as they solve difficult problems and inspire their people to work hard in achieving their divine goals.

The Holy Spirit unites people together to accomplish a specific mission. The main goal of any leader is to unite people in a spirit of harmony and peace to work with all their might to accomplish great things. These are the words recorded by Doctor Luke, concerning the conduct of the Church after Pentecost: "All the believers were one in heart and mind."[75] Unity of minds and actions is the fruit of the Holy Spirit.

The Holy Spirit inspires a leader to action and commitment in serving his fellow men and accomplishing God's purpose. Action is the source of influence in the life of a leader. You will know a leader filled with the power of the Holy Spirit when they are constantly working and elevating man to do great things for people and God.

The Holy Spirit impacts lives. Jesus was the spring of life to the people. Leaders are followers of Jesus. Leaders filled with the Holy Spirit likewise become a spring of life to the people. Leaders are life givers and healers. The main goal of any leader should be to give life to people.

The Holy Spirit gifted some specific leaders with prophetic gifts, like Daniel, to encourage and prepare the people for the future of their work.

Conditions for a leader to receive the Holy Spirit

A leader must be born of the water and Spirit. This means that the leader must accept and surrender his life to God through baptism—immersion in the water like Jesus in Jordan. Cory Wetterlin made this powerful comment: "Only through surrender can transformation occur."[76] The Spirit of the Living God occupies the minds of the one who surrenders to be led by God. The Spirit of God works through the revealed Word of God in your life. Acceptance of the Word of God allows His Spirit to renew your inner person — born of the Spirit.

A leader must keep feeding in the Word of God daily. When the rain falls on the ground, it is possible for the plant to absorb nutrients from the soil and manufacture its food. The same with the Holy Spirit—He is like rain that falls in the soil of your heart and makes it possible for your inner spirit to absorb the Word of God and manufacture its spiritual food to nourish your spirit to grow in the likeness of God.

A leader must accept God's commission in their life. Each one of us has a part to play in lifting mankind to greatness, according to God's will. Do your part.

A leader must cultivate heavenly thoughts. The leader must cultivate thinking good thoughts that will elevate his soul to communion with God daily. Meditating on the Word of God will cleanse the soul from the corruption of this wicked world.

A leader must maintain the burning desire to serve his fellow men. The Spirit of God was given to us to lead our fellow men in knowing God, to live better and enjoy the blessings that God created for all of us.

A leader must live with people in the spirit of harmony. If possible, live with everyone in perfect peace. The Spirit of God does not dwell in disunity and disharmony. The Holy Spirit does not live in the heart of a leader who harbors envy and hatred against his brethren. Those who devote themselves in loving and promoting peace are the true temple of the Holy Spirit.

SPECIAL ABILITIES

To these four young men, God gave knowledge and understanding of all kinds of literature and learning. And Daniel could understand visions and dreams of all kinds.[77]

The king talked with them, and he found none equal to Daniel, Hananiah, Mishael and Azari; So, they entered the king's service. In every matter of wisdom and understanding about which the king questioned them, he found them ten times better than all the magicians and enchanters in his whole kingdom.[78]

Now Daniel so distinguished himself among the administrators and the satraps by his exceptional qualities [excellent Spirit] that the king planned to set him over the whole kingdom.[79]

Then King Nebuchadnezzar fell prostrate before Daniel and paid him honor and ordered that an offering and incense be presented to him. The king said to Daniel, surely your God is the God of gods and the Lord of kings and a revealer of mysteries, for you were able to reveal this mystery.[80]

Then the king placed Daniel in a high position and lavished many gifts on him. He made him ruler over the entire province of Babylon and placed him in charge of all its wise men. Moreover, at Daniel ask, the king appointed Shadrach, Meshach and Abednego administrators over the province of Babylon, while Daniel himself remained at the royal court.[81]

Then at Belshazzar's command, Daniel was clothed in purple, a gold chain was placed around his neck, and he was proclaimed the third highest ruler in the kingdom.[82]

God blessed Daniel and his colleagues with knowledge, understanding and wisdom. God endowed Daniel with special gifts of understanding visions and dreams. In the Babylonian empire, people considered dreams vital for the kingdom's survival. Dreams revealed impending war or calamity, so the people could prepare for the future. If the king received a dream, they took this as a message from the gods. The ruler surrounded himself with priests, diviners and astrologers to interpret whenever the king received a dream he could not understand.

We see Daniel reveal and interpret the dream in chapter 2, and the king makes him governor of the province of Babylon. At the request of Daniel, King Nebuchadnezzar places the friends of Daniel to administrative positions in Babylon.

Daniel accomplished this task because God endowed him with this special gift of interpreting dreams. God blessed Daniel with the ability to interpret dreams as a gift to benefit the king of Babylon, his empire and the world. The king placed Daniel in the highest position in the province of Babylon because of his ability to interpret dreams and solve difficult problems.

Daniel solves another mystery in chapter 4. King Nebuchadnezzar had another dream, and nobody could interpret it or give it meaning. Daniel was summoned to give the interpretation of the dream, because of his ability to understand dreams. He resolved the mystery and earned respect and honor from the king.

Besides all this success, Daniel gave the interpretation of the writing on the wall during the reign of Belshazzar, and he was honored as the third highest person in all the kingdom in Babylon. Wealth and resources were placed on him, though he did not want them, because he knew the kingdom was ending.

We can define special abilities as doing things with extraordinary capacity that cannot be achieved with general intelligence. As we discussed earlier, Daniel could interpret dreams and visions which were vital for the survival of the kingdom. This capacity was possessed only by Daniel among his colleagues, which made him extra useful to the king. It placed Daniel in the most powerful positions in the land that gave him great influence in the kingdom and the world.

Leaders who aspire to influence a great number of people in the world today must possess special abilities. Think about it—if you're an employer and you have 10 individuals with the same education and qualifications looking to gain the same position you are offering, what kind of process will you adopt to select a suitable candidate? No matter what kind of selection process you use, it will boil down to one principle: you will choose an individual who has special abilities that will benefit your organization or company with greater influence.

Special abilities come in two categories. The first category is those abilities you develop by obeying the natural laws of God until they become magic. For example, if you're a teacher, to distinguish your work from the rest of the team, you cultivate a special ability to connect with your students on their level. This places you in a special position among the students and your fellow teachers.

In a business setting, you study your market in depth and you come up with a process that meets the needs of your customer in such a way that your competitors cannot compete with you at the same level. This may be a simple service like packaging, connecting with the customer, well-trained employees or product delivery. The general rule is that special abilities give you an edge in serving your followers.

A Christian can obey and follow all the requirements presented in Scripture and following the commandments of God by faith in Jesus. By doing so, their life will shine compared to the rest of the team. These are laws that are obeyed in the natural world—if you plant a tree and take care of it, by abiding with the law of nature, the plant will grow well compared to those that have been denied a suitable environment to grow and flourish.

A leader could advance their skills by taking a special course that gives them unique abilities to solve a problem that their fellow leaders lack. That training that gives you a special skill in a certain area of your profession and distinguishes you from another employee.

The second category of special abilities comes as a gift from God. No matter how you try to copy the individual endowed with it by applying all the laws of God, nothing will happen. Yes, these abilities are given because an individual has developed all the natural talents as given by their Creator, but now, the Creator complements his efforts with divine gifts to accomplish greater things for God and their fellows.

Some abilities are given as a gift at birth—there is nothing you can do to copy them. Some individuals are set apart for special work from their birth— you cannot imitate them. God gives gifts according to His wisdom and abundant grace to His people. Some are given more, some are given less, all for the purpose of building His people.

Leaders who train in the school of Jesus, when they see that an individual is blessed beyond their abilities, do not hinder them by trying to destroy their work, but help them achieve more and do more, because they know special abilities that the Lord has endowed are given for a purpose. This means they will hold a high position to exact greater influence on the world.

Special abilities empower the leader to hold a high position of authority. This may be formal or informal; it gives the leader the lever he needs to exercise power to do good for his fellow men. It's divine for leaders to desire and develop themselves to hold positions of power. If the position of power is occupied by an individual who is well-disciplined and loves the Lord and people, great things will happen.

The higher you ascend in positions of power, the greater the responsibility, but it comes with greater privilege to influence people. Your creativity increases as you ascend to the position of power and authority; the challenge with a lower position is that it denies you the benefit of exercising your brain to create and make decisions that will influence a greater number of people.

Your superiors tell you what to do and not to do; this prevents you from having the freedom to create things that sometimes will not work but provides you with valuable insight about the future assignment. The leaders must seek ways to help themselves have the freedom to try new ideas, and sometimes they will succeed and sometimes fail.

The testaments of the Bible's leaders endowed with special abilities

Joseph had an ability to interpret dreams. There was no one in Egypt that could interpret dreams like Joseph. First, he interpreted the dream of two prisoners, which paved the way two years later to interpret the dream of Pharaoh. After Joseph explained the meaning of the dream, the king found no one to have a keener mind and more wisdom than Joseph. So, he made Joseph a prime minister of Egypt and prepared the country to survive with a famine that lasted seven years.

God favored Moses to talk to him face-to-face, as man talks to his friend. This privilege gave Moses the opportunity to present his problems and the difficulties of his people to God and to receive an answer without delay. Moses was endowed with a mysterious power that made his face shine like the sun. This made Moses receive honor, respect and fear from the children of Israel.

God gifted Deborah, Elijah, Elisha, Isaiah, Jeremiah, Ezekiel and many more with prophetic abilities, to build up and guide their fellow men to worship and honor their Creator. The gift of prophecy is given to edify and build the family of God and to warn them when they go astray from the Holy Scripture. The gift of prophecy is not given to everyone, but to specific individuals. Through their hard work and commitment, we all benefit.

The shadow of Apostle Peter could heal people as he passed through the street. Apostle Paul's handkerchief touched sick individuals, and they were healed. God blesses some people with special abilities, for special assignments in fulfilling the divine purpose.

OVERSHADOWED WITH GOD'S FAVOR

Now God had caused the official to show favor and compassion to Daniel.[83]

Daniel, you who are highly esteemed, consider carefully the words I am about to speak to you, and stand up, for I have now been sent to you.[84]

Do not be afraid, you who are highly esteemed, he said. Peace! Be strong now be strong Daniel, you who are highly esteemed, consider carefully the words I am about to speak to you, and stand up, for I have now been sent to you. And when he said this to me, I stood up trembling.[85]

A farmer goes out in the morning and in the evening, sowing seeds; it's the duty of the farmer to prepare the ground, to choose good seeds and plant them in the right seasons. Also, it is the duty of the farmer to take care of the plants, root out weeds and ensure the best environment for the plants to grow.

After the farmer has done his work, the rest he leaves to the Creators, to shower rain from above, to quicken life inside the seeds and to sustain him until the plants grow and bear fruit, without understanding the intricacy of how life works inside the plant.

The same principles apply in self-development and personal success. It is our duty as leaders to plan, prepare and take necessary steps that lead to prosperity, and leave the rest in the hands of the Lord. The Lord will favor our work by showering his blessings on us to ensure success in our endeavors. The favor of God comes to those prepared to receive His blessings. Preparation is the prerequisite to receive—no preparation, no receiving.

After we have done all that in our sphere as leaders, the rest we leave with the Creator. He will touch the people to open the door for us; He will open opportunities where there were no opportunities; He will open opportunities to receive financial help and guidance from His angels to aide us in our work, and they will work in moving the hearts of men.

As the farmer rests and sleeps, knowing that he has done all that he can, so the leader rests knowing that he has done his best. Our mandate as servants of the Lord is to work with all our hearts and leave the results with the Lord. We should not be concerned with the results beyond doing our best—the Lord will worry about the results.

Therefore, preparation is vital in the leader's life, and because preparation involves planning, it is wise to strategize. Planning involves designing small steps that lead toward achieving the main aim of the organization or individual.

For example, a leader plans to read one book a month, and this month they choose a book on leadership that contains 200 pages. The leader writes the goal on a sheet of paper and writes all the results he expects to achieve at the end of the project. The leader writes how they will feel after finishing the project, including emotions like accomplishment, competence, courage and satisfaction. Finally, they visualize and see how it feels to achieve that goal. Now, the question is, how to achieve this aim?

The next step is for the leader to assess the available resources that will help them achieve their goal. In addition, they assess the resources they do not have but are needed to achieve the goal. For example, in our case, the leader will need a quiet place, time, concentration, money to buy the book, a store to buy the book, good health, discipline and maybe some motivation from a friend or book club.

The leader starts with the end in mind, moving backward to the beginning. 200 pages divided by four weeks equals 50 pages, divided by seven days a week comes to approximate seven pages per day. Now the goal is more achievable. They just have to read seven pages per day to finish the book in the month. It takes an average of half an hour to finish seven pages. So instead of browsing Facebook for half an hour a day, the leader sacrifices that half an hour of browsing Facebook and develops their leadership skills.

Steps to achieve your goals

The leader creates a specific picture in their mind of what they want to achieve in a specific time frame. The beginning of great things in a leader's life is creating an inspiring picture in their head. The image you have in your head about yourself and the future will materialize.

The next step in achieving your goal is to write it down on paper. Writing your goals commits you to work and persist to achieve it. Draw the picture you have imagined in your head; make a blueprint of your plans. A contractor draws the blueprint of the structure he is about to build. It helps to clarify the details and specifications of the plan.

The leader visualizes the goal to create the feeling of what could be if they achieve their goal. Visualizing your goal fires your body into action. When you visualize your goal, it helps to see it in your head and commit it to long-term memory, so that when you see an opportunity that will help to achieve that picture, you do not delay in taking action.

The leader identifies the resources needed to realize the goal. The leader must identify resources they need to achieve the ambitious goal and other resources to make the goal a reality.

Breakdown the goal to yearly, monthly, weekly, daily and hourly. This makes the object clearer and achievable. A goal must be specific, timely and realistic. A journey of 1,000 miles starts with one step. Here, the leader sets a time to begin the work to achieve their noble goal. Time helps the leader and their followers measure and reflect how much they have accomplished and how far they still need to go.

The leader decides what sacrifices he will give up achieving the goal; the leader must calculate the cost that he or she must pay to achieve their goal. Nothing comes without paying the price. Most of us fail in life because we are not willing to pay the price for what we want. We reap what we sow; the measure that we put into work is proportional to what we will harvest.

Now the leader requires discipline to achieve the objective. They may require some assistance in achieving their objective, like joining a book club or finding a reading partner. After the month is over, the leader reflects on the results of the initiative, learns from it and motivates themselves to achieve more.

In a team setting, a group of six Canadians planned a vacation to climb Mount Kilimanjaro on August 1, 2019; it takes a week to reach the summit. They sit down and discuss all the benefits they will gain by climbing Mount Kilimanjaro and collecting pictures of being on top.

First, they choose a leader. The leader assigns all tasks according to individual's abilities and availability and ensure everyone is happy with their position.

The leader consults a guide, who gives them the weather conditions, what kinds of clothing they need, what kind of food, the cash they need while they are in Tanzania. He gives them all the hotel options and

prices, security conditions, medical requirements and
the physical preparation required by all climbers.

They decide that this project is worth achieving; they
check on the two-way fare from Canada to Tanzania.

"Daniel and his friends placed themselves where
God could bless them."[86] It is our work to place ourselves
where God can pass His blessing to us, so we can share
with others.

Our minds must be in a state to receive God's
blessings. Open your heart wide to receive God's
blessings. God will not give that which you have not
conceived in your mind. How can you appreciate His
gifts if you did not expect Him to fulfill His promises?
Expect great things from God. Expect abundance and
live in expectance that God will bless your work and
open opportunities for you to prosper; sing songs of
praise that God is blessing you.

We must serve with faith that God will bless us.
God has created us to serve our fellow men with a heart
of gratitude. Faith will open the windows of Heaven to
shower us with blessings and favor. With faith, every
promise of God is fulfilled. With faith, you flourish in
loving service to your followers. By faith, believe that
God is blessing your work.

We must obey what God asks us to do. Every promise
from God is attached with a condition. The conditions
demand our perfect obedience.

Obey His Word and claim His promises. It's our duty
to claim the promises of God. God is waiting for His

children to claim His promises with faith. Meditate on God's promises and you will receive. Open your mouth wide, and God will fill your treasury with Heaven's treasury. It's the longing of our heavenly Father to fill our house with good treasure, both temporal and eternal. The more the leader claims God's promises, the more God opens their mind to see more opportunities. Work and plan with all your knowledge and use the available resources God provides. Depends on Him with all your heart for His blessings.

In Eden, it was the duty of Adam to work and take care of the garden, and God crowned their work with blessings and favor from above. The vivid example we have as Christians is the life and work of Jesus Christ, how he took advantage of opportunities presented before him. He spoke words of life to those who wanted to hear, he healed the sick, comforted the broken-hearted, encouraged those who were giving up on life, ministered to the needy, fed the hungry, visited the sick and empowered men to be better and grow in fullness of life as God provides. We can learn from Christ by how he took advantage of the opportunities presented before him.

Another critical point I have learned from the life of Daniel is that he made all his decisions ahead of time, before they happened. Distinguish yourself by always planning. Opens your inner eyes, gaze into the future and see opportunities before they become reality.

Remember, when an opportunity becomes a reality, you are late.

RECAP | PERSONAL LEADERSHIP:

To recap what we have learned about personal leadership, it's wise to look into the life and ministry of Jesus. When Jesus came to this world to save mankind from the degeneration of sin, he established values that provided direction on how to carry out his mission and conduct his daily life. The values he established gave him singleness of purpose and the wisdom to eliminate activities which contribute nothing to his mission. Here are Jesus's values, as recorded on the scroll of Isaiah 61:

(Anointed:)

To proclaim good news to the poor.
To bind up the brokenhearted
To proclaim freedom for the captives
and release from darkness for the prisoners
To proclaim the year of the Lord's favor
And the day of vengeance of our God.
To comfort all who mourn.
And provide for those who grieve in Zion
to bestow on them a crown of beauty
instead of ashes;
The oil of joy
instead of mourning;
a garment of praise

instead of a spirit of despair;
Oaks of righteousness a planting of
The Lord for the display of his splendor.

Now, my question to you is: what is in your personal values? Have you allowed others to determine values which do not fit into the mission and work that God have given you?

Because of the values that defined his mission, Jesus always looked upon difficult moments with a positive attitude (proactive mind). How could he improve the situation? How could he bring healing to individuals? When he saw hungry and marginalized individuals, he always asked how he could feed them and bring hope.

He offered his life to be a channel of blessings to mankind. His mindset was serving others with humility and love. He expected much from his Father, and he received abundance to bless his fellow men. Now, ponder for a moment—are you the light and salt of the world? When the time comes to give up your last breath and be put to rest, what will be spoken of you by those around you? What will be your legacy?

To make his mission effective and infectious, and to make his ministry continue in his absence, Jesus selected and fostered mutual friendship for the purpose of influencing the world with the Gospel. So, he chose 12 disciples to follow Him wherever he went, to learn from him and support him in his work.

Now, if you want to run faster, run alone and get forgotten like a flash of lightning; but if you want to endure for decades after you rest with your ancestors, walk with wise men. Who are your friends? Are they inspiring you to be better or are they dragging you to the path of self-destruction? It's my prayer that the Lord gives you understanding on this principle.

To solidify his friendship with his disciples and to connect with his Father, he devoted countless hours in prayer. These were chosen hours of the day. Prayer is the source of strength and power. A man who knows to wait in prayer will always stand any adversity.

To serve man with excellence and humbleness of mind, Jesus always devoted his heart, mind and body to understanding the Word from his Father, as well as understanding the needs of his followers and those he came to minster. The insights gained gave him wisdom to serve people and touch them where they needed him the most. Understanding will preserve you wherever you are called to serve. My question to you is: are you intentionally learning to understand your fellow men?

For this purpose, Jesus submitted his whole being to the influence of the Holy Spirit. The Holy Ghost filled Jesus with knowledge, insight, understanding and wisdom to create better methods to serve mankind. Have you devoted enough time to understanding the workings of the Holy Spirit, as presented in Scripture? The Spirit of God endowed Jesus with special abilities—

the power to heal, to raise the dead, to teach the Gospel and to do miracles that are beyond human imagination.

Because of the beautiful work that Jesus did, he was favored in the sight of man. As he humbled himself unto death on the cross, his Father favored him and made him ruler of everything visible and invisible, King of kings, Master of the universe. How powerful will it be if we follow the example given to us by our Savior?

CHAPTER 5

PROBLEMS

SOLVING DIFFICULT AND COMPLEX PROBLEMS

Leaders exist to solve problems. If there were no problems, we would never need leaders. A leader fills the void that exists in his followers in their search for meaningful lives filled with prosperity, peace, harmony and growth for the future. Every problem that a leader solves creates new benefits and increases the happiness of society as a whole. Leaders must have a correct perspective about problems. Understanding the meaning of a problem will change the entire perspective of a leader to better thinking and attitude on services and life itself.

Now we come to the core of our discussion on solving problems. We will discuss the steps Daniel undertook to solve the mystery of the forgotten dream. First, it is important to define the meaning of a problem with a correct perspective of our discussion. According to Merriam-Webster's dictionary, "problem" means, **"obstacle."**

A problem is an obstacle that needs to be overcome by a leader to move on to the next stage of his development. A problem is an obstacle between you and glory and honor. Karen Martin, in her book *Clarity First*, says: "A problem is merely a gap between where you are and where you would like to be or need to be."[87] Let's say you have a certain result you would like to achieve, but to achieve it, you may have to produce more products or work harder.

Problems are blessings in disguise; the moment you solve them, you receive your blessings. It is paramount that a leader must learn how to solve difficult problems as they come. Solving problems is the work of a leader. Solving a problem requires skills. If the problem is complex, it requires a high level of thinking and understanding to connect the dots to resolve the problem.

Solving difficult problems requires the right attitude and good training. Daniel was the man for the occasion. He had all the skills needed to explain the meaning of the dream. To Daniel, this was an opportunity for promotion, to shine for his people and to bring honor to his God. All the training Daniel received through guidance from his God came to use. The lessons we learned in previous chapters now come to play; we will see how Daniel applies the skills he gained in leadership training.

CASE I: SOLVING THE MYSTERY OF FORGOTTEN DREAM

King Nebuchadnezzar dreamed while in his bed. When he woke in the morning, he could not recall the dream. They valued dreams in the ancient empires as messages from the gods concerning the survival and prosperity of the kingdom. If disaster were to fall on the nation, the message was passed through dreams from gods. The messages hidden in the dream were expected to be interpreted by a priest, astrologer or other men who were connected with the gods. Kings surrounded themselves with witches, scientists, priests, historians, chanters, magicians, enchanters, sorcerers and prophets.

The king summoned the wise men in his palace to tell him what the dream was and the interpretation of it. At first, Daniel and his friends were not included among the counselors with the king, maybe because they were junior in their service or maybe because of the jealousy of their Chadian comrades.

The king explained to them the cause of the call; he gave them time to seek what the dream was and the interpretation of it. After searching, using all means available to solve the mystery, they went with disappointing news to the king that they could not solve the problem. Gods that live among men could not give an interpretation of the dream, but perhaps gods that live not in the realm of men could.

The king was furious because the enlightened men could not reveal the dream or its interpretation. He gave them another opportunity to figure out the problem, or else all of them would be killed by sword, because they had teamed up to deceive the king. After they could not solve the mystery, the king issued a proclamation to kill all the wise men in Babylon. The task of annihilating the wise men was given to a man called Arioch, "the messenger of death." In going to execute the judgment, he went to execute Daniel and his friends. Let's see the manner in which Daniel dealt with the problem:

Step 1: Daniel meets with the messenger of death, Arioch.

Arioch went out to kill all the wise men of Babylon. In the cause of his mission, he met with Daniel, who was not aware of the dream the king's advisers failed to interpret or that the king issued a decree to kill all the wise men.

This is the plight that Daniel found himself in the presence of the messenger of death. The reason that Arioch came into Daniel's court was to kill him and his companions. The moment Daniel met with the messenger of death was a deciding moment for him either to live or to die. This was an opportunity presented to Daniel in the form of a threat of death. Had Daniel lost his temper or become fearful, we would never talk about him now. Had he lost his state of mind and acted arrogant, he and his colleagues would have died with the wise men of Babylon.

Many times, opportunities present themselves in a disguised form. They may come to us as hardship, disappointment, irritation from friends, loss of a loved one and pain. In any form opportunity presents itself, we must accept it as a gift, because we never know if that is the hour of breakthrough.

This is the moment that training is vital. When you meet with imminent danger, it is human nature to flee from danger. We must train ourselves to keep calm in any situation, no matter the case. If we are to die, we will die no matter what we do. Pain will come if it must come. Learning to trust God is vital in such circumstances, and it does not come easy. We must learn to trust God and His promises. Now we are approaching the problem that depends on our training, wisdom and tactics.

Step 2: Daniel uses tactics and wisdom to understand the problem.

When Arioch, the captain of the king's guard, had gone out to put to death the wise men of Babylon, Daniel spoke to him with wisdom and tact. He asked the king's officer. Why did the king issue such a harsh decree? Arioch then explained the matter to Daniel.[88]

The messenger of death came to kill; disobeying the command of his master was a sure path to his own death. Going back to the king to say he had not performed the task was suicide.

Merriam-Webster's dictionary defines "tactics" as "the science and art of disposing and maneuvering forces in combat. Or can be defined as the art or skill of employing available means to accomplish an end." Daniel used wisdom to apply his tactics. Dictionary.com defines "wisdom" as "the soundness of an action or decision regarding the application of experience, knowledge, and good judgment."

Let's imagine you met with a general who had sworn to kill you. What would you do? What did Daniel do? This is how Daniel dealt with the officer who was sent to kill him: Daniel asked a question to understand the problem. Why did the king issue such a harsh decree? If Daniel had fled, they would have killed him. If Daniel lost his composure and panicked, he could not explain himself and would have been killed.

There are three things Daniel did. Firstly, **Daniel calmed himself**. When you're peaceful in facing difficulties, your brain works efficiently. In the face of this danger, Daniel maintained his balance of mind.

Secondly, **he offered the honor and respect deserved by the officer**. Men crave respect, and when they meet with an individual who respects their work and position, their humanity kicks in—the desire to preserve life and help his fellow men to enjoy the blessing of life with humbleness and humility. But what if Daniel disrespected the officer? He would not last for a second. Respecting men of authority will give you an opportunity to express your ideas before they get rid of you.

Thirdly, **Daniel asked to understand the nature of the problem**. The question that Daniel asked the messenger of death shows how much he wanted to understand. As the messenger of death explained the problem to Daniel, Arioch's fury subsided in explaining the reasons for the decree. There is something natural that happens to the heart of a man that calms him down when afforded an opportunity to explain himself, no matter the position of power.

Understanding the problem helped Daniel decide what his next move would be. Understanding will preserve the leader. If you do not have clear insight into the problem, you will make a blind decision that will lead you to destruction.

Step 3: Daniel requested the king for time to seek the meaning of the dream.

At this, Daniel went into the king and asked for a time, so that he might interpret the dream for him.[89]

Some problems can be solved instantly; some need time to be understood. It took almost 10 years for Albert Einstein to experiment and comprehend the theory of relativity of time. This applies to our daily lives as well; there are problems that need effort and special abilities to gain insight required to explain them. Wise leaders know the value of time when it comes to dealing with difficult problems that need a solution to ensure the survival and prosperity of the entity, they are leading.

If you fail to solve a problem in the right moment as required by the law of nature, opportunity will slip by, and sometimes lives will be lost. It is critical to solve a problem in the right season and implement the right solutions.

Giving an incorrect solution to a problem will produce destruction, especially in the matter of leading a country—dealing with matters of life and death. It's better to take a longer time to seek a better solution than hastily resolve a problem and apply wrong solutions. Understanding this principle, Daniel knew that the problem the king was trying to solve required time and a special revelation from God.

Daniel, with wisdom and tactics, requested the king give him some time to interpret the dream. The king granted him the opportunity to seek solutions wherever they could be found. Daniel found favor in the king's sight—that is why he was given time to seek the meaning of the dream. During the interview of Daniel and his friends, the king found them to be smarter than the rest of Chadian students.

As a leader, it's vital to build trust in any ordinary moment gained with men of authority; when a critical moment comes, you will find favor. In a critical moment like this, you need favor from men of power and God to ask a special favor. The special favor may be financial support, time to seek solutions (like in the case of Daniel), to be granted authority to accomplish a task or recommendations. The trust you build with your coworkers and superiors is like a bank account—every time you deposit a penny, it grows in so much that when the moment comes to withdraw, you always have plenty to rely on.

Step 4: Daniel goes to his home and explains the problem to his mutual friends.

Then Daniel returned to his house and explained the matter to his friends Hananiah, Mishael and Azariah.[90]

The next step after he earned the favor was to find the tools to solve the problem. For Daniel, he went to his house and shared the matter with his colleagues. In their discussion, they found that they could not solve the problem by either reading books, experimenting or consulting other experts on the issue. There was only one way to solve the problem—to seek God's wisdom.

Here is the importance of having a group that you can share your troubles with. Solving difficult problems like Daniel faced requires a union of like-minded people. You cannot stand in critical moments with a divided group of leaders.

There are problems that will be solved just by consulting your friends. The importance of joined effort is indispensable in our modern world, where challenges emerge with various faces every day. These problems require diverse techniques to solve. Scientists say that one brain has over two billion neurons; if you have three people, you have six billion neurons. You have increased the capacity three times compared to one individual. The whole is greater than the individual parts that form the union. During conversations like that of Daniel and his colleagues, it produces valuable insight into solving complex problems.

Step 5: Daniel encourages his friends to seek God's wisdom in prayer.

He urged them to plead for mercy from the God of heaven concerning this mystery, so he and his friends might not be executed with the rest of the wise men of Babylon.[91]

After an intense discussion, the only way to solve the problem was through prayer. Daniel encouraged his friends to seek God in earnest prayer. People despise the necessity of prayer in solving difficult problems, but for Daniel, it was another way to consult the intelligent Beings of Heaven. One habit of a leader at a personal level is prayer. Seek God with faith in prayer. When people of the same values unite in prayer, seeking wisdom to solve a problem, it will preserve life and bring blessings to the world—Heaven is moved with compassion and love.

Burning one candle produces a little light, but when you burn multiple candles, the light grows bigger and bigger. When our hearts unite in the spirit of cooperation in seeking God, it delights Heaven. God creates both female and male to unite in working to bless each other. Daniel understood this principle very well; instead of praying in private alone, he encouraged his friends to pray together.

Another reason we seek God in prayer together is because the challenges we are facing affect us all. We all must feel the need to seek God in prayer. We must face the challenge as a team. When the Lord reveals the solution, we may share the joy of the fruits of our work.

Step 6: Daniel and his friends trusted that God would answer their prayers.

After presenting your case before God, you must trust that He heard and will answer you according to His abundance of mercy. These leaders, after they have poured their hearts to God, claim the promise that the Lord has given them. They trusted that the Lord would honor and bless them.

Mistrusting the promises of God is a sin, and dishonors God because He has assured you He will bless you according to His Word. As the book of Hebrews states, "faith is confidence in what we hope for and assurance about what we do not see And without faith it is impossible to please God, because anyone who comes to him must believe that he exists and that he rewards those who earnestly seek him."[92]

With this promise, these young men went to sleep with peace of mind, knowing that somehow the Lord would fulfill His promise. It demands a lot of training to relax when the stakes are high.

Step 7: God reveals the dream to Daniel in a vision during the night.

During the night, the mystery was revealed to Daniel in a vision.[93]

God revealed the dream and interpretation of the dream while Daniel was asleep. Why did the Lord appear to Daniel while asleep? The main median that the Lord has ordained to communicate with His servant is through the physical brain that hosts the center of consciousness, intelligence and spirituality.

Our brain and body work best when we are relaxed completely. We can only discern the voice of God when all other voices have been silenced. When we are occupied with the cares of this world, it diminishes that still voice in our hearts.

Most times, prophets and leaders receive revelations while asleep. God spoke to Abraham after he fell into a deep sleep. God appeared to Solomon and asked him what He should do for him in a dream. God appeared to Peter when he was napping in the upper room in a dream.

This insight is vital for leaders to learn how to sleep effectively—relax and calm down their physical body, while tuning their heart to their Creator, expectantly waiting to receive a revelation from God. The question is: how can you as a leader learn to rest in such a way that God can communicate dreams and visions while rejuvenating your body? What techniques will enhance your sleep so you can connect with God?

Your work as a leader is to search out ways to tune your mind to that still voice in your heart. Most powerful leaders have mastered the wisdom to shut off the world around and connect with the influence of the Holy Spirit, the revealer of all wisdom and knowledge.

Step 8: Daniel praises God for revealing the mystery to him.

The character of a man is revealed when he achieves his object. Will he turn and give glory to the One who helped him achieve his goal? Daniel proved to be a man of integrity and honor by praising his God, who, according to His mercy and grace, revealed the dream to Daniel.

Then Daniel praised the God of Heaven and said:

Praise be to the name of God for ever and ever;
Wisdom and power are his.

He changes times and seasons;
he deposes kings and raises up others.
He gives wisdom to the wise
and knowledge to the discerning.
He reveals deep and hidden things;
he knows what lies in darkness,
and light dwells with him.
I thank and praise you, God of my ancestors:
You have given me wisdom and power,
you have made known to me what we asked of
you,
you have made known to us the dream of the
king.[94]

He praised his God for giving him wisdom and insight to understand the dream. Daniel gave praise to God, who is in control of everything that happens in Heaven and under the heavens. When he gave praise, he acknowledged that God did not reveal the mystery because he was somehow wise compared to the rest of his colleagues, but because God was merciful.

Praising God gives the leader an attitude of gratitude and humbleness of heart to stay connected with the source of all knowledge and wisdom.

Step 9: Daniel goes back to the messenger of death and requests to be presented before the king.

Then Daniel went to Arioch, whom the king had appointed to execute the wise men of Babylon, and said to him, "Do not execute the wise men of Babylon. Take me to the king, and I will interpret his dream for him."[95]

Arioch took Daniel to the king at once and said, "I have found a man among the exiles from Judah who can tell the king what his dream means."[96]

Daniel did not run to the king directly to present his case; rather, he went first to Arioch, the man who was given authority to kill all the wise men in Babylon. This is the man who gave Daniel favor by preserving his life and disobeying the command of the king so that Daniel could ask for time to seek the solution of the mystery. This shows how Daniel understood how men of authority work. Had Daniel ignored him, he would have to pay a heavy price later in his leadership.

Some of us, the moment we get what we want, do not remember those who made a ladder for us to climb to the top. We forget those who sacrificed their golden opportunity for us to shine. We ignore those who risked all for our success, offered their financial aid or a place to lay our heads when we were struggling to make ends meet. We burn those bridges that should be kept open; no one has an idea of what lies ahead.

Humility is an attribute that leaders foster. Because of humility, they achieve great things in life; they never brag or despise those who are under their leadership. Humility reminds us we are human, and we depend on the help of others to get ahead. So even when we are mistreated and humiliated, we dust our pride off and be grateful to those who are not generous to us.

How relieved Arioch must have felt when Daniel presented himself before him with eyes glowing with confidence, requesting to be presented to the king to give him the interpretation. Instead of killing innocent people, now he was to bring a redeemer to the king.

Also, Arioch was thrilled because he had found a solution for the problem which had troubled his master. Remember, the mission of Arioch was to be a solution to his master, so he would do anything to make his master happy. A leader like Daniel would strive to be a man of solutions to his master. Having these skills will open doors which would have never been opened otherwise.

Step 10: Daniel honors his God before the king.

Daniel replied, no wise man, enchanter, magician or diviner can explain to the king the mystery he has asked about, but there is a God in heaven who reveals mysteries. He has shown King Nebuchadnezzar what will happen in days to come. Your dream and the visions that passed through your mind as you were lying in bed are these.[97]

Instead of Daniel taking all the glory and honor before the king, he honors his God in Heaven. Some of us feel uncomfortable giving glory and honor to God, who has shown us the path of life; instead, we brush away the idea of praising our God before great men, because we feel that they will not honor us. This is being dishonest to ourselves and God. The reason for this is human pride.

To understand the effectiveness of this principle, let's look the death of Herod, recorded in the book of Acts:

*Then Herod went from Judea to Caesarea and stayed there. He had been quarreling with the people of Tyre and Sidon; they now joined together and sought an audience with him. After securing the support of Blastus, a trusted personal servant of the king, they asked for peace because they depended on the king's country for their food supply. On the appointed day Herod, wearing his royal robes, sat on his throne and delivered a public address to the people. They shouted, this is the voice of a god, not of a man. Immediately, **because Herod did not give praise to God**, an angel of the Lord struck him down, and he was eaten by worms and died.[98]*

Step 11: Daniel uses effective communication skills to speak to the king.

Daniel applied effective communication skills in delivering the solution to the king. We will discuss this topic in depth in a chapter on communication.

Step 12: Daniel is honored by the king and appointed as the governor of the province of Babylon.

Then King Nebuchadnezzar fell prostrate before Daniel and paid him honor and ordered that an offering and incense be presented to him. The king said to Daniel, surely your God is the God of gods and the Lord of kings and a revealer of mysteries, for you were able to reveal this mystery. Then the king placed Daniel in a high position and lavished many gifts on him. He made him ruler over the entire province of Babylon and placed him in charge of all its wise men.[99]

Special skills open doors for greater opportunities to lead. God favored Daniel by revealing the dream and interpretation to him. The king honored him by appointing him as the governor of the province of Babylon.

Daniel did not refuse the opportunity because he knew that the Lord had opened that door for Daniel to serve Him with honor in a high position. The more authority you have, the greater the influence. The main purpose of a leader is to educate himself as much as they can and to desire to hold the highest position in any capacity possible to achieve great things for God. Whenever these opportunities open, we must take advantage of them. This does not mean that we should take on so much responsibility that our spiritual and intellectual development is hampered. Wise leaders know their limits.

God cooperates with men to do His works and bring the fulfillment of His promises to His people. Nebuchadnezzar was a servant of God in his position as a king, but he was not fully aware of his responsibilities before God. For God to influence his mind to know His purpose, He brought Daniel closer to him. The revelation of the dream and interpreting it was a means to make the king conscious to the guidance of the King of kings.

Step 13: Daniel requests the king honor his friends.

Moreover, at Daniel's requests the king appointed Shadrach, Meshach and Abednego administrators over the province of Babylon, while Daniel himself remained at the royal court.[100]

After the king honored Daniel, Daniel never forgot his comrades. Daniel knew the power of having friends that share the same values and principles. He honored his friends who cooperated to seek God in prayer for the revelation of the dream.

Daniel was not selfish; he was generous in his heart. We must imitate Daniel's character in our endeavor to become influential leaders. Leaders bring others along as they climb to the top. Being at the top is more enjoyable with your friends. The main goal of a leader is to open doors for others to shine.

Daniel knew that his personal growth and public leadership would be enhanced by nurturing his friendship with his inner group and to seek a possible position that would bring them closer to him. This strategy would help him solve difficult problems because he could always go to them for advice and encouragement. If you're alone at the top of a mountain, it is very lonely up there; but with others, it's enjoyable and empowers you to climb more mountains.

CASE II: THE AUTHORITY AND POWER OF GOD | MAN'S STRUGGLE FOR POWER AND GLORY

Every problem requires a different strategy to solve it. Wise leaders study the nature of the problem and find ways of solving it, according to their uniqueness.

I, Nebuchadnezzar, was at home in my palace, contented and prosperous. I had a dream that made me afraid. As I was lying in bed, the images and visions that passed through my mind terrified me.

So, I commanded that all the wise men of Babylon be brought before me to interpret the dream for me. When the magicians, enchanters, astrologers and diviners came, I told them the dream, but they could not interpret it for me. Finally, Daniel came into my presence and I told him the dream. (He is called Belteshazzar, after the name of my god, and the spirit of the holy gods is in him.) I said, Belteshazzar, chief of the magicians, I know that the spirit of the holy gods is in you, and no mystery is too difficult for you. Here is my dream; interpret it for me. These are the visions I saw while lying in bed: I looked, and there before me stood a tree in the middle of the land. Its height was enormous. The tree grew large and strong and its top touched the sky; it was visible to the ends of the earth. Its leaves were beautiful, its fruit abundant, and on it was food for all. Under it the wild animals found shelter, and the birds lived in its branches; from it every creature was fed. In the visions I saw while lying in bed, I looked, and there before me was a holy one, a messenger, coming down from heaven. He called in a loud voice: Cut down the tree and trim off its branches; strip off its leaves and scatter its fruit. Let the animals flee from under it and the birds from its branches. But let the stump and its roots, bound with iron and bronze, remain in the ground, in the grass of the field. Let him be drenched with the dew of heaven and let him live

*with the animals among the plants of the earth.
Let his mind be changed from that of a man and
let him be given the mind of an animal, till seven
times pass by for him. The decision is announced
by messengers, the holy ones declare the verdict,
so that the living may know that the Most High
is sovereign over all kingdoms on earth and gives
them to anyone he wishes and sets over them the
lowliest of people.*[101]

Step 1: The king asks Daniel to interpret the dream because of his special abilities.

The king expresses disappointment because the magicians and astrologers failed to interpret the dream. At this moment, the king addressed Daniel with his credentials as the chief of all wise men in Babylon. It seemed Daniel presented himself before the king after hearing the problem that troubled him and the dilemma he was experiencing.

The king trusted Daniel because of his special abilities, granted to him by the Holy Spirit. "Belteshazzar, chief of the magicians, I know that the spirit of the holy gods is in you, and no mystery is too difficult for you. Here is my dream: interpret it for me."[102] The king knew Daniel because of his ability to interpret dreams. Remember, Daniel already interpreted a dream for the king in Daniel chapter 2.

The special ability here, **interpretation of dreams**, caused the king to ask Daniel to give the explanation of the dream. God granted this special ability to Daniel through the working of the Holy Spirit. The ability that Daniel possessed gave him the credibility to explain the vision. His authority over the king came because of his talent that no one else in the kingdom possessed. When you are gifted to solve difficult problems, people do not have a choice but to respect and protect you. Doors to corridors of power are open to those who are endowed with incredible power (intelligence, wisdom, understanding) to give solutions for hard problems.

The goal of a leader is to influence as many people as possible; to achieve this objective, they must be positioned at the highest post in the system as possible. If you climb the highest mountain, the better the view compared to that underneath you.

But the winds at the highest point are violent and dangerous, and breathing is difficult. Sustainability at the top of the mount requires tremendous skill; that is why most of us are not willing to pay the price to tackle the climb. The only path to shine and impact the world is with the glory of God.

Step 2: Daniel pays attention as the king explains the problem to him.

While the king explained his problem to Daniel, Daniel never interrupted the king. He paid full attention to the details. A crucial skill to be owned by a leader at any level.

Step 3: Daniel took some time to respond to the king.

After the king had explained the dream to Daniel, Daniel was perplexed for a time. While the king explained the dream, Daniel understood the principle underlined in the problem and what it meant. He was filled with the Spirit of God, and the Spirit gave him insight to understand the dream.

The Spirit of God gives wisdom, insight and understanding to solve difficult problems. Jesus said, when the Spirit of God comes to you, He will lead you to the whole truth as proceeding from the mouth of God.

The Spirit of God can only explain the wisdom of God. Leaders submit themselves to the leadership of the Holy Spirit. By doing so, God communicates His wisdom to them. The only channel between God and mankind is His Holy Spirit. Because the Spirit of God lived in Daniel, the meaning of the dream was revealed to him.

Daniel took some time to arrange his thoughts and ideas to effectively achieve the greatest outcome. At the same time, he wanted to speak to the king with wisdom.

Leaders spend ample time preparing before they present their solutions to their followers.

1. They prepare their hearts and minds for maximum effect.
2. They make sure they understand the topics they want to present.
3. They study their audience's psychology and readiness to receive the message.
4. They arrange their ideas to reflect the weight of each idea.
5. They foresee the climax and intended outcome of their message.

Step 4: Daniel prepares the king's heart to receive the interpretation of the dream.

This how Belteshazzar answered, "My lord, if only the dream applied to your enemies and its meaning to your adversaries!"[103] Understanding the weight and impact of the dream, Daniel did not start by telling the interpretation directly. He started with something the king would like to hear. Though Daniel understood very well who the dream applied to, he did not shoot the arrow directly at the king first.

The psychological impact of this strategy is that it lowers the listener's shield down and opens the door for you to penetrate their heart. Effective salesmen recommend that as you present your product to your prospects, the first answer should be a yes, which will give you another yes. When the time comes to lead them to commitment, no matter how hard it is, you're likely to get a final yes.

Recommendations that a leader can adopt in presenting new ideas or in persuasion:

1. Start with something that will give you a yes from your audience. Then lead them to the idea that requires difficult decisions.
2. Start with known to unknown.
3. Target the soft flesh before hitting the heart. Your goal is to influence the heart, but remember, the heart is very sensitive to direct attack.
4. Avoid starting with controversial ideas in the beginning of your presentation. Controversial ideas create opposition that lasts.
5. A leader is a farmer who softens the soil before digging.

Step 5: Daniel retells the dream to the king.

The tree you saw, which grew large and strong, with its top touching the sky, visible to the whole earth, with beautiful leaves and abundant fruit, providing food for all, giving shelter to the wild animals, and having nesting places in its branches for the birds Your Majesty, you are that tree! You have become great; your greatness has grown until it reaches the sky, and your dominion extends to distant parts of the earth. Your Majesty saw a holy one, a messenger, coming down from heaven and saying, cut down the tree and destroy it, but leave the stump, bound with iron and bronze, in the grass of the field, while its roots remain in the ground. Let him be drenched with the dew of heaven; let him live with the wild animals until seven times pass by for him.[104]

Why does Daniel retell the dream to the king?

1. To assure the king, he understands the problem well.
2. To make sure he understood the problem well.
3. To show that he cares, and he paid attention when the king was explaining the dream.
4. To give credibility to his interpretation and solution.

Step 6: Daniel interprets the dream.

This is the interpretation, Your Majesty, and this is the decree the Most High has issued against my lord the king: You will be driven away from people and will live with the wild animals; you will eat grass like the ox and be drenched with the dew of heaven. Seven times will pass by for you until you acknowledge that the Most High is sovereign over all kingdoms on earth and gives them to anyone he wishes. The command to leave the stump of the tree with its roots means that your kingdom will be restored to you when you acknowledge that Heaven rules.[105]

1. Daniel never sugarcoated the meaning of the dream, he told it as it is **(integrity)**.
2. Daniel spoke the truth with courage despite the cost associated with the king understanding the dream. **(authenticity)**.
3. Leaders do their work and leave the results to God. **(maturity)**.

Step 7: Daniel finishes his interpretation by giving counsel.

Therefore, Your Majesty, be pleased to accept my advice: Renounce your sins by doing what is right, and your wickedness by being kind to the oppressed. It may be that then your prosperity will continue.[106]

Note, Daniel did not push his ideas on the king. He used polite language: "be pleased to accept my advice." Most leaders miss this remarkable strategy, because they know the solution, so everyone should buy into it—that is not always the case. After Daniel gave his suggestion, the king did not act on it; he continued in his arrogance until the day the Ruler of everything said enough is enough, and the dream was fulfilled.

Be courageous enough to accept that people have their own choices and always bend to follow their inclinations. As a leader, when you have done all that you can, go thy way and rest.

SUMMARY OF THE ABOVE STEPS

1. **Your position of authority or your reputation will give you the mandate to solve complex problems in your profession (Identifying the problem).**
   a. The opportunity to tackle a specific problem comes because of the special abilities endowed to you by God or through training and determination.

2. **Understanding the problem is the key to solving it (understanding).**
   a. Every problem presents its own uniqueness.
   b. Every problem presents its own principles and opportunities to be uncovered.
   c. Listening with keen minds to absorb every detail is vital to unearth the treasury buried beneath the mystery.

3. **Take some time to prepare yourself (reflection).**
   a. Prepare your thoughts and ideas according to weight of their impact on your audience.
   b. The time you take to prepare will depend on the complexity of the problem.
   c. Internalize the impacts of your solution to the audience.
   d. Understand the psychology of your audience.

4. **Prepare the heart of your audience (pre-imple-mentation).**

   a. Understand the weight and impact of the meaning of the dream. Daniel did not start by telling the interpretation. He started with something the king would like to hear. Though Daniel understood very well who the dream applied to, he did not shoot the arrow directly to the king first.

5. **Retell the problem to your audience with your own words (credibility).**

   a. This shows you care for your audience.

   b. Reassure your audience that you understand the problem.

   c. Ensure that you understand the problem.

6. **Interpret the problems (designing).**

   a. Explain the underlying principle that holds the meaning and application to the problem.

   b. Explain the opportunities that are presented by the problem.

7. **Advice or counsel (implementation).**

CASE III: WRITING ON THE WALL | YOUR KINGDOM IS TAKEN FROM YOU

One day, King Belshazzar, the grandson of King Nebuchadnezzar, held a great banquet for great men of his kingdom and his concubines. During the period of celebration, he commanded the vessels of the temple of God be brought to be used in drinking. He did this as an act of arrogance because he knew the customs concerning the vessels. No one could use them except during religious services. If you remember, his grand-father, Nebuchadnezzar, acknowledged the God of Heaven as the supreme leader in the affairs of men; King Belshazzar knew of the sacredness of the temple vessels, so using them was an act of rebellion against the God of Heaven.

While they were in a high spirit of festivity, Belshazzar saw handwriting on the wall that he could not understand or interpret. All the wise men were summoned to explain the meaning of the words on the wall. Seeing that no one in his kingdom could interpret the meaning of the words, fear gripped everyone in the room. Because of the fear, they shouted and made many noises. They knew this was an act of God.

Due to the commotion, the queen heard the noise going on in the room, and understanding the source of disturbance, she spoke with the voice of confidence that there was a man who could interpret the meaning of the inscription on the wall.

The reason that the queen was not in the banquet is not explicitly explained; perhaps she was a worshipper of the Living God. She was not in favor of what was going on in the palace hall.

The king understood Daniel's moral standard; he may have not wanted to include Daniel in his admin-istration. This was perhaps the cause as to why Daniel was not in the banquet hall.

Step 1: Recommendation of Daniel's special abilities.

The queen, hearing the voices of the king and his nobles, came into the banquet hall. May the king live forever! she said. Don't be alarmed! Don't look so pale! There is a man in your kingdom who has the spirit of the holy gods in him. In the time of your father he was found to have insight and intelligence and wisdom like that of the gods. Your father, King Nebuchadnezzar, appointed him chief of the magicians, enchanters, astrologers and diviners. He did this because Daniel, whom the king called Belteshazzar, was found to have a **keen mind and knowledge and understanding, and the ability to interpret dreams, explain riddles and solve difficult problems. Call for Daniel, and he will tell you what the writing means.** So, Daniel was brought before the king, and the king said to him, are you Daniel, one of the exiles my father the king brought from Jud? I have heard that the spirit of the gods is in you and that you have insight, intelligence and outstanding wisdom. The wise men and enchanters were brought before me to read this writing and tell me what it means, but they could not explain it. **Now I have heard that you are able to give interpretations and to solve difficult problems.** If you can read this writing and tell me what it means, you will be clothed in *purple and have a gold chain placed around your neck, and you will be made the third highest ruler in the kingdom.*[107]

Step 2: Daniel refuses gifts from the king.

In Daniel chapter 2, Daniel accepted gifts from King Nebuchadnezzar; not only does he take the gift, he also recommends his friends be trusted with positions of power.

This time, Daniel takes a different path: "Then Daniel answered the king, you may keep your gifts for yourself and give your rewards to someone else. Nevertheless, I will read the writing for the king and tell him what it means."[108]

1. Leaders are not motivated to serve because of gifts they receive from their followers or superior. Leaders accept gifts that will enlarge their service to their fellow men.

2. Leaders understand there is a time to receive and a time not to receive.

3. Leaders are wise enough to know that some gifts add nothing to their mission. So they refuse to receive them.

Step 3: Daniel explains the root cause of the problem.

Every problem facing humanity carries principles that govern the meaning, the solution and the blessing. Maybe the problem was caused by disobeying the laws of nature, or the problem drew your attention to a principle that, if obeyed, will add success to your endeavor. The moment you are aware of the problem, that is just the tip of the iceberg; its connection is composed of small chains of events, choices and the decision that lead to the challenge.

For-example, if you discover a crack in the wall, the crack is the visible problem, but the cause may not be visible. The joints were possibly not connected properly, the soil underneath the foundation is not stable (soft) or the foundation was not built according to structure codes. Sometimes the materials used to build the walls are not constructed to withstand pressure from the structure.

Identifying the cause of the problem leads to finding the right solution. Most individuals run to fix the visible problem without taking time to consider the source, only to realize that they have made the problem bigger. The work of a leader is to lead his people to understand the principle that makes up the challenge beforehand.

Sometimes, the problem is like an iceberg in the ocean. Skilled ship captains understand that when they see an iceberg, it is a small portion of the bigger structure. The ocean covers a bigger problem than what they see. They measure the size of it so they do not run into it. An iceberg is the accumulation of small chunks of ice that solidified together. The problem Daniel was dealing with was an iceberg. Here is how he dealt with it:

Your Majesty, the Most High God gave your father Nebuchadnezzar sovereignty and greatness and glory and splendor. Because of the high position he gave him, all the nations and peoples of every language dreaded and feared him. Those the king wanted to put to death, he put to death; those he wanted to spare, he spared; those he wanted to promote, he promoted; and those he wanted to humble, he humbled. But when his heart became arrogant and hardened with pride, he was deposed from his royal throne and stripped of his glory. He was driven away from people and given the mind of an animal; he lived with the wild donkeys and ate grass like the ox; and his body was drenched with the dew of heaven until he acknowledged that the Most High God is sovereign over all kingdoms on earth and sets over them anyone he wishes. But you, Belshazzar, his son, have not humbled yourself, though you knew all this. Instead, you have set yourself up against the Lord of heaven. You had the goblets from his temple brought to you, and you and your nobles, your wives and your concubines drank wine from them. You praised the gods of silver and gold, of bronze, iron, wood and stone, which cannot see or hear or understand. But you did not honor the God who holds in his hand your life and all your ways. Therefore, he sent the hand that wrote the inscription.[109]

Step 4: Daniel explains the
meaning of the writing.

This is the inscription that was written: mene, mene, tekel, upharsin.

Here is what these words mean:

Mene: *God has numbered the days of your reign and brought it to an end.*

Tekel: *You have been weighed on the scales and found wanting.*

Peres: *Your kingdom is divided and given to the Medes and Persians.*[110]

Step 5: Daniel is rewarded and made the
third highest man in the kingdom.

Then at Belshazzar's command, Daniel was clothed in purple, a gold chain was placed around his neck, and he was proclaimed the third highest ruler in the kingdom. That very night Belshazzar, king of the Babylonians, was slain, and Darius the Mede took over the kingdom, at the age of sixty-two.[111]

RECAP | SOLVING DIFFICULT
AND COMPLEX PROBLEMS:

1. Leaders exist to solve problems, and to empower their followers to unite their efforts to solve the problems facing their communities.

2. A problem is merely a gap between where you are and where you would like to be.

3. Problems comes in all forms and shapes.

4. Use tactics and wisdom to understand a problem. Each problem is unique, it requires innovation to solve it.

5. Each problem has its own solutions; if one solution does not work look for another one.

6. No matter how big the problem is; remember, all things are possible with God.

7. Remember for every problem you solve, the people who are benefited by your wisdom will reward you. Do not forget to honor God and those who helped you to achieve your success.

8. If the problem is too difficult to understand now, give yourself time to seek out a solution, never be quick to devise solutions for the problems if you do not have complete understanding.

9. It is wisdom for a leader never to force people to adopt his solutions. If people do not want to follow your lead now; in many cases, you may have to let it go until such time they come to understand your point of view.

10. Leaders cultivate their abilities day by day, so that when a problem presents itself, they are ready like Daniel.

CHAPTER 6

SUPERIORS

DEALING WITH PERSONNEL OF POWER AND AUTHORITY

Whether you're a CEO or junior leader trying to develop or advance your leadership skills, you will interact with people endowed with power and authority either by trust from their followers or because of their extraordinary skills. Man, by nature, is selfish and self-centered. They have a longing to be admired and respected proportional to their authority and power.

As a leader, you want to develop a system that is effective in dealing with them, so they don't hinder your leadership development or ideas, but open doors for you to advance to the fullness of your potential and hard work. Everyone has people who oversees their work. As president of a nation, the people who voted you into power are watching how you conduct your work, and your cooperation with them will ensure your longevity.

We have seen Daniel, as a leader in a foreign country, find himself under the leadership of kings who did not fear God. But Daniel did not complain or murmur; instead, he designed ways to communicate and work with them. Many times, in your leadership, you will have to work under men who neither fear God nor obey His laws. It doesn't matter who is your boss—what you need is to develop a system to lead in partnership with them.

A distinguishing characteristic of leaders who fear God is that they develop better ways of dealing with their fellow leaders, whether they are believers or non-believers. Jesus had to deal with Rome's leaders who ruled Israel during his mission here on Earth.

Paul and other apostles had to preach and present the Gospel to great men of power and authority who never feared God. Joseph had to lead with Pharaoh and his officers, who were not worshippers of God.

We have the testimonies of great leaders who governed their countries harmoniously while partnering with heathen kings: Nehemiah, Abraham, Isaac, Jacob and Moses. It's vital to learn how to work with people of power and authority regardless of their faith and beliefs.

Remember, when you are working with people of authority, you are dealing with their varied temperaments and habits. Some leaders have developed poisonous behaviors that can hamper your leadership and development. Some have very strong personalities that are hard to deal with. Whether the behavior is inborn or the product of choice, you need skills and wisdom to serve with personnel of authority.

In this section, we will learn various techniques Daniel deployed in dealing with men of authority and power. Remember, Daniel was a governor of the province of Babylon, chief of wise men under Nebuchadnezzar's reign, and vice president under the reign of Darius. Daniel had vast wisdom to counsel us on how to work with men of power.

PRESENT YOUR IDEAS AND REQUESTS WITH FIRMNESS, BUT NEVER APPEAR FORCEFUL

Therefore, Your Majesty, be pleased to accept my advice: Renounce your sins by doing what is right, and your wickedness by being kind to the oppressed. It may be that then your prosperity will continue.[112]

Daniel then said to the guard whom the chief official had appointed over Daniel, Hananiah, Mishael and Azariah, please test your servants for ten days: Give us nothing but vegetables to eat and water to drink. Then compare our appearance with that of the young men who eat the royal food and treat your servants in accordance with what you see. So, he agreed to this and tested them for ten days. At the end of the ten days, they looked healthier and

better nourished than any of the young men who
ate the royal food. So, the guard took away their
choice food and the wine they were to drink and
gave them vegetables instead.[113]

We feel powerful and intelligent when we make decisions according to our own terms and judgment. As you work with people at personal or professional levels, you notice that people do not change because of scientific lectures. People love to cling to their own ideas, opinions and idioms. People love for their ideas and beliefs to be affirmed by others. This is one factor that makes it difficult to influence people to follow your ideas.

If you are working under someone's authority, it's obvious that you need to use tactics and wisdom to change their opinion. Perhaps trying to alter your superior's behavior to follow your suggestions will arouse their ego and they will deflect you and cripple your leadership development.

God created us with individual power to choose and decide. The moment we meet with people trying to change us, we feel that they are attempting to control and belittle us. It requires wisdom and tactics to bring your ideas across. Many times, when a junior leader finds their boss stiff to bend to their suggestions or proposals, they find other ways to carry out their objectives or try to outsmart their boss.

The moment you try to outsmart your master, you create an atmosphere of competition. The sense of competitiveness on your part will stimulate your boss to fire their arrow against you. This becomes more dangerous when you are more gifted than your leader.

I will say: never try to outmaneuver your boss. Some people will say, "Then how can I get ahead?" You do not advance by undermining the authority of your supervisors, but by helping them shine even more:

> When you're dealing with your boss: never tear him or her down; help them grow strong. If you want to accomplish greats projects in a large bureaucracy, get inside your bosses' heads. Expect what they want before they know they want it. Take on their problems; make them look so good that you become indispensable. When they can't get along without you, they will support anything you seek to accomplish.[114]

Your goal is to find a better way to make them shine, in so much that their success depends on you. Whenever they goes, they should feel safe with you. You want your boss to depend on you, because of your skills and strong character.

Your actions and integrity will make your boss respect you with the whole of their being. You want them to cherish you more. When the time comes for them to retire, they will recommend you as their successor. At a young age, focus on developing your reputation and talents; prepare yourself. When the opportunity appears, you will be ready.

How do you make your boss decide to favor you or grant you the desire of your heart? Know both your boss's strengths and weaknesses; complement their weakness without others noticing and let them receive praises and honor because of your work.

Help make their talents more visible to followers; speak highly of them in their absence. Let surrounding people know that you respect and obey your boss. These must come from your heart. The moment your superior feels complete in your presence and vulnerable in your absence, there is no limit of how far you will go.

RESPECT AND HONOR YOUR SUPERIOR'S POSITION OF POWER AND AUTHORITY

Daniel answered, May the king live forever![115]

Your majesty[116]

Belteshazzar [Daniel] answered, my lord, if only the dream applied to your enemies and its meaning to your adversaries![117]

A major need of man is to be loved, appreciated and esteemed as a unique creature endowed by the Creator with special abilities and responsibilities. People are dying because of desire to be esteemed by others. People desire to be king over others. To feed this need, people try all kinds of crazy things to achieve this, by taking bold actions and creating better ideas/theories to prove their inherited intelligence. Many inventions by man are to prove to others that they are comparably superior. We hate to be ruled. We want to be ruler of ourselves.

We find significance in our work. We feel elevated when we perceive that our work improves the lives of others. We devote tremendous energy and resources to developing those skills that will make us successful in our career.

Fruit of our hard work comes as others trust us with roles that set us apart as leaders. Being a leader in any capacity fills that need of respect and honor engraved on our hearts. When our followers and partners respect our efforts, despite our shortcomings, it opens our heart to give and give and give again.

When our subordinates disrespect our work or role, it triggers our heart to resent them and close. Because we are leaders in making, we depend on others to pave the way for our growth; we must supplicate this longing of heart to our superiors.

A few things you can do to achieve this goal

1. Genuinely learn to support your superior to succeed. Everything starts from the heart. Fill your heart with thoughts geared to support your superior. You will need to alter your pattern of finding fault; focus on finding good in your supervisor. Dig deep

and find their strengths; learn and study ways to succor their projects.

2. Understand your superior's talents and gifts, so you can help them shine and achieve great things. Understanding is the key. Knowing the potential of your leader, their abilities, will help overcome the sin of pride. Everyone has weaknesses and short-comings; no one is perfect. Concentrating your energy on the potential of your superior will give you a new, positive perspective on your boss.

3. Respect the title of their position as required by your organization. Any system that you will work under will have established titles to each position. This is to make sure distribution of tasks is carried out according to the needs of the organization, supported with authority and power. The system ensures that decisions are made befitting the needs and established rules. Respecting people's title is vital and biblical. Temptation comes when the hold of the position is arrogant. Be patient, leader-in-making, because the title has less to do with the behavior of the individual rather than the system that established the position. If you respect your boss's position of authority and title, people under you will do the same.

4. Never badmouth your superior. The easy way to vent your hatred against your boss is to badmouth them. This will harm your reputation more than taming your tongue. If you have nothing good to speak

about your boss, keep it to yourself—if you destroy their reputation, the reports will reach eventually them. They will do you harm or you will never find favor in their eyes.

5. Always speak highly of your superior. Keeping quiet is good, but not always. Open your mouth wisely, speak of your superior talents, achievements and aspirations. When this news reaches their ears, they will love you and respect you. The greatest outcome of honoring your superior with your tongue is that your audience will respect and trust that you will do the same for them. By doing this, you are planting seeds of greatness.

6. To control your emotions, the best strategy is to spend time in prayer, praying for your superior. Pray that God will give them success in their work. Pray that they find joy in their service to others. Pray that God gives you wisdom to deal with them despite their weakness or shortcomings. Pray that God opens their eyes to see your contributions and trust you with more work and responsibility. Remember, the work that we do is to be measured by God. If you do good work, he will exalt you like Daniel, Moses, Joseph, Esther and Nehemiah. The crown waits for those who love from the heart.

7. Through your work ethic, win the heart of your superior. Your character, faith and the motives of your heart are revealed through your works. Works are the fruit of who you are.

EARN YOUR SUPERIOR'S RESPECT
THROUGH YOUR WORK ETHIC

At this, the administrators and the satraps tried to find grounds for charges against Daniel in his conduct of government affairs, but they could not do so. They could find no corruption in him, because he was trustworthy and neither corrupt nor negligent. These men said, we will find no basis for charges against this man Daniel unless it has something to do with the law of his God.[118]

Trust is a fabric that unites people together and causes them to think as one mind. Trust takes time to develop. In cultivating a friendship with your mentor, you need character. If your character is not suitable to be trusted, it will hinder your growth.

Any leader is interested in producing results. Your mentor and superiors exist because of producing the best products or catering the best service. "If your bosses see you lifting burdens off their shoulders, and they find out they can trust you, they stay out of your face. And they give you the freedom you need to operate independently and improve your ship."[119] Their success depends on their ability to produce. They will rejoice if they find a leader-in-making who strives to produce; they will be delighted to support them to succeed.

To be trusted, you must be trustworthy. Privately cultivate integrity in your heart, especially when you are alone. It's hard to pretend to be trustworthy before people; you can sometimes fool people, but not forever. Being faithful in small ways will makes you faithful in great things.

Enjoy hard work and create effective ways to be productive. You must purposefully cultivate a positive attitude toward work. Love what you do with all your heart. Your supervisor will love you because of your positive attitude. Positive attitude toward work and your coworkers will open doors for your personal growth and advancement. Consider your work to be a blessing and gift from the Lord.

Foster integrity rather than quick gains. The greatest temptation for many leaders is to seek quick gain. The moment your overseer perceives that you are susceptible to quick gain, they will never place you in a position of power and authority; they know that the moment you ascend to a position of authority, you will get rid of them to enrich yourself. It's better to let others know that they can trust you as the sun rises every morning.

Seek to be better in anything your hands find to do. In chapters 2-3, we learned that you must cultivate your talents and be a master in your field. Let your followers and your superiors know that you are well-equipped to do your job—they will overlook other shortcomings of yours.

Learn to cooperate with others in your organization. Organizations succeed because of the compounded effects of accumulated talents. People build organizations. Learning to work and live with others in perfect harmony will increase your desirability in your organization. Promote others, and they will promote you. Appreciate other people's achievements, and they will do the same for you. Focus on aiding others to accomplish their projects.

Be a problem solver, not an incubator of division. Focus your energy on solving problems in your organization, which will contribute to the success of your organization. They hired you, to support your boss solves problems; commit to that goal. If you allow yourself to be distracted, you may utter unwanted ideas that brings division among your colleagues.

Love beauty in everything you do. If you love beauty in your work, it will foster and encourage creativity in your work. Creativity is the product of loving beauty in its natural form. Seek beauty in everything that your hands do. Find beauty in your teammates.

Seek understanding more than anything else; act with discernment. Never open your mouth without understanding; seeking to understand people. Refer to chapter 4 for techniques on acting with understanding rather than assumptions—the major block in developing lasting relationships with others.

POWERFUL LEADERS ARE JUST HUMANS—DUST AND ASHES

One thing that humbles us all is the immanency of death. Death chooses neither rich nor poor, literate or illiterate. When it comes, it takes its course. This should make us humble.

Great leaders like pharaohs, Nebuchadnezzar, Alexander the Great and Napoleon Bonaparte are all dead. Their bones and flesh have perished and turned to dust. What remains is their legacy—nothing more.

Great leaders experience pain, fear, loneliness, hunger and thirst; they get sick. They are mortal. The things you love are the same things they love.

We should never get scared of them as if they are gods. They are flesh and blood. Some of them are not gifted compared to you. What set them apart is their authority in the community.

The position of authority comes with power. The Word of God encourages us to respect and honor them. The position gives them a mandate, and if you are not wise, they can destroy your leadership development prematurely, before you reach your full potential.

Because of their role in an institution or country, we must respect and honor them. They are working to improve our lives. They work for the interest of us all. They may look less gifted compared to you, but the position gives them a mandate to exercise power and authority over you. It's appropriate that you respect and honor them.

Another commanding reason is that leaders are enthroned by God to work on His behalf. Whenever we respect and honor them and help them do their work, God is pleased because we are honoring Him. Here is the Word of God through King Nebuchadnezzar, after being humbled by God: "Most High is sovereign over all kingdoms on earth and gives them to anyone he wishes."[120] When they disobey God, He punishes them, rooting them from the position of power.

Leaders ought to obey God more than regular men. We must Honor his commandments more than any other. In chapter 3 of Daniel, the three companions of Daniel disobey the command of the king to worship the idol he made. With rage, Nebuchadnezzar threw them into a furnace. But God rescued them from flames.

They threw Daniel into the den of lions because of his faithfulness to the King of kings. God rescued Daniel from the hungry lions. There are no limits to what God can accomplish with his mighty hands.

Finally, never trust flesh and blood; trust the mighty hand of God, and you will be secure like His throne.

DEALING WITH EGO, PRIDE AND EGOCENTRIC LEADERS

"Ego," according to the Oxford English Dictionary, means: "A person's sense of self-esteem or self-importance." Each person has a certain level of ego that helps us keep our sense of self. If we did not have it, we would live as empty machines. The problem comes when we do not use our conscious mind to control these feelings. If these feelings are not subdued, they develop to adulthood and become a disease, which may bring destruction to you.

"Pride" is defined as: "A feeling, or deep pleasure or satisfaction derived from one's own achievements, the achievements of those with whom one is closely associated, or from qualities or possessions that are widely admired." Also, if pride is not kept in check, it will lead to self-exaltation and create a false opinion of one's position of power.

An egocentric leader is someone who thinking only about themselves and what is good for them.

Signs of egocentric leaders:

1. Speaks only about their success as a source of power and authority.
2. Believes only in their own ideas and intelligence.
3. They are arrogant and ignorant in understanding others.
4. Authority and power only revolve around their decisions.
5. Their ego is fragile when challenged by others on their opinions and ideas.
6. Their needs are first, not the other way around.
7. They force their perceived truth onto others. Their way alone is to be followed.
8. They are envious because of insecurity within themselves.

If you are working with a leader who has a fragile ego, deal with them with care; any move that threatens their power and influence will hurt your leadership development. You will endure a bigger problem if your leader is egocentric. The earlier you diagnose the problem; you will be able to deal with it strategically to avoid unnecessary confrontation that will cripple your leadership development.

Nebuchadnezzar, Saul, Judah and Cain are a few leaders from Scripture that proved to be egocentric. For illustration, God told Cain and his brother Abel what kind of sacrifice to offer, with clear instructions of what they should offer to be accepted in the sight of God. But Cain followed his own way, and God did not accept his sacrifice. Abel's offering was accepted.

Cain, instead of taking responsibility for his rebellion, hated his brother Abel, shifting the blame to his brother, as if he had offered the same sacrifice as he had. Had Cain obeyed the voice of God, his offering would have been accepted. But look what happened: "Then the Lord said to Cain, 'Why are you angry? Why is your face downcast? If you do what is right, will you not be accepted? But if you do not do what is right, sin is crouching at your door; it desires to have you, but you must rule over it.'"[121] Cain never paid attention to the voice of God, and he followed the same rebellious spirit which led him to disobey his Creator.

God warned Cain of his evil attitude, and the sin that was encroaching on him if he did not control his thoughts. Cain failed to subdue his evil feelings about his brother and he planned ways of eliminating his brother: "now Cain said to his brother Abel, 'Let's go out to the field.' While they were in the field, Cain attacked his brother Abel and killed him."[122] This is the goal of egocentric leaders—to kill and eliminate people who possess character that is superior to theirs.

Another poisonous trait of egocentric leaders is that they never take responsibility for their actions, or rarely try to correct their evil behavior; the safe pass for them is to defend themselves and to look good before others. Pay attention to the conversation between Cain and God after Cain killed his brother: "Then the Lord said to Cain, 'Where is your brother Abel?'"[123] Cain responded to the Creator God, "'I don't know,' he replied. 'Am I my brother's keeper?'"[124] This answer shows his arrogance—he shifts his blame to God. He never took responsibility for his own actions, even shedding the blood of his own brother.

The all-knowing God, with Spirit of love and humbleness, uttered this word of wisdom: "What have you done? Listen! Your brother's blood cries out to me from the ground. Now you are under a curse and driven from the ground, which opened its mouth to receive your brother's blood from your hand. When you work the ground, it will no longer yield its crops for you. You will be a restless wanderer on the earth."[125] The Creator of the universe, and the creator of Cain, tried to help Cain recognize his wrongdoing. The only way was to pronounce punishment on the evil Cain had done.

Cain was not concerned with seeking forgiveness; he cared only for his position of power and his safety. Cain said to the Lord, "My punishment is more than I can bear. Today you are driving me from the land, and I will be hidden from your presence; I will be a restless wanderer on the earth, and whoever finds me will kill me."[126] There is no remorse for the pain he had inflicted on his own brother. To him, pain was not for him, but others, to suffer. Had God not intervened, Cain would have been happy and enjoyed his life.

Leaders, this story offers us a very practical lesson—reflect on it, seeking God's wisdom to understand it, and when you understand what kind of person you're dealing with, you will succeed.

To change such a person is hard, almost impossible. My advice to you is: trying to change these types of leaders directly will only hurt you; use an indirect strategy. If it does not work, leave them alone. Keep praying for them. Even God Himself could not change Cain, He left him alone. The only thing God did was love him and extend His mercy and grace.

Lessons from Daniel on dealing with egocentric leaders

1. Though Daniel was the wisest man in the entire kingdom, he never bragged about it:

As for me, this mystery has been revealed to me, not because I have greater wisdom than anyone else alive, but so that Your Majesty may know the interpretation and that you may understand what went through your mind.[127]

2. Daniel claimed his success to God, never to himself:

I thank and praise you, God of my ancestors: You have given me wisdom and power, you have made known to me what we asked of you, you have made known to us the dream of the king." Daniel replied, "No wise man, enchanter, magician or diviner can explain to the king the mystery he has asked about, but there is a God in heaven who reveals mysteries.[128]

3. Daniel never tried to change his superior ego, but left it for God to deal with: Many times, we think we can change self-centered leaders, but our effort goes unnoticed, and if we are not careful, we get hurt by these consuming fires of insecurity in the leader's heart. Leave the work of changing people to God. Win them over through your character and influence.

UNDERSTAND THE "INS AND OUTS" OF THE SYSTEM

To be an expert in any area, you need to learn the system and know it in depth. Let us say you want to be a successful auto mechanic. Your task will be to study and master each part that makes the car a complete system and learn how they work as one unit to make the car useful.

As a leader-in-making, your task is the same as an auto mechanic. You need to understand the organization that you are working under. You need to know who is whom. You need to know which department contributes what in the system, which department is the pillar to the whole organization. Sometimes it may appear that the president holds the power, but the actual power lies somewhere else.

You need to know the behavior of the people who work in the organization, from the lowest position to the CEO or president. You need to know how to navigate bureaucracy. You need to know who holds the key to the whole thing. You need to know which door to enter and where it leads. You need to know the system and become the system in knowledge and understanding.

A few suggestions on learning the system:

1. Know your role in the organization. They created the system for you and the interest of everyone involved in the system. It is important to understand with depth the limits and power of your position, so you do not interfere with others and your superior. Stepping on ground that is not yours will create fire; this may impede your leadership development and advancement.

2. Learn and know in-depth your strengths and weaknesses. Your strengths will give you means to understand the system. For example, if you are gifted in reading books, then it will be wise to read all the

manuals available to you in order to understand the system. If you are good at connecting with people, then talk with people tactfully to understand the system in depth.

3. Learn from experts. Spend time with those who know the system. It takes time to create systems, and it involves a great number of experts. To understand it, connect with them and ask them questions. Ask effective questions that will lead you to figure out the system. Observe with keen eyes how they relate with each other, how they communicate with people and how they fix machines. This will bless you with a great treasure.

4. Remember the system is not mechanical or brick-and-mortar, it's comprised of people. The key to the whole thing is to know and serve people. People create systems and product. Love people and serve them, and it will amaze you how much the system opens to you like a book.

5. It takes time to know things and be masters. Do not rush. Patience is the key to attaining anything in life. You will never know everything at once; it will take tremendous energy and commitment to master the system step-by-step.

6. The aim of learning and mastering the intricate of the system is to be an effective leader in your work. Your purpose is not to manipulate the system but to be a blessing. Sometimes, you may have to destroy the legacy system to create a new one. But to create

a new system, the old one gives you a beginning point. We do not create from nothing; we create from something. What you have now is either bad or good; thank God for the blessing through it, and you will gain wisdom to create a better one.

EVERY KINGDOM COMES AND GOES

Everything under the sun comes and goes. People are born, grow, lose the beauty of youth and age, and then die. Trees grow, dry out, fall and decay. You cannot avoid the force of the laws of nature; they don't perish. They stay forever—only things and people decay.

Kingdoms come and go. The kingdom of Babylon came and is no more; the same of the Persian and Median. The Greek conquered the world in a short amount of time; it's buried in ashes today. The mighty Roman empire ruled the world with iron fist, but it too disintegrated and is no more.

This insight helps us to keep our pride in check. Your existence today does not grant that you will be here tomorrow. Nature can take its course, and you will be no more. The system that you are working in may disappear tomorrow or change to something new that you never expected. As a leader-in-making, make sure you maintain flexibility and allow yourself to adjust without losing your core values.

Remember:
1. Change and time are constant.

2. Moral laws (treat your fellow men with love) and the laws of nature have never changed since the beginning of man.

3. God and His Word live forever. God said the sun would rule during the day and the moon would rule the night. This law has never changed.

4. Those who put trust in God's promises will live forever. God promised Noah that He would never destroy the Earth by a flood again. This promise was confirmed by the rainbow, still ruling today.

5. You will not remain the same forever. Whether you like it or not, you are the testimony of this law. Compare yourself from a few years ago to today.

6. We create things, and they depreciate and disappear. Cars rust and waste way. Your clothes decay and waste away.

7. Today, you're rich and tomorrow everything could be taken away from you. Now, you may be rich in life, but sooner or later, it will be taken away.

Wise words from King Solomon

There is a time for everything,
and a season for every activity under the heavens:
a time to be born and a time to die,
a time to plant and a time to uproot,
a time to kill and a time to heal,
time to tear down and a time to build,
a time to weep and a time to laugh,

a time to mourn and a time to dance,
a time to scatter stones and a time to gather them,
a time to embrace and a time to refrain from embracing,
a time to search and a time to give up,
a time to keep and a time to throw away,
a time to tear and a time to mend,
a time to be silent and a time to speak,
a time to love and a time to hate,
a time for war and a time for peace.[129]

RECAP | DEALING WITH PERSONNEL OF POWER AND AUTHORITY:

1. Remember as you develop your leadership skills; you will work under leaders who are endowed with power and authority. You must develop a thoughtful strategy to deal with them.

2. Sharpen your observation skills so you may distinguish those supervisors who are motivated by ego and pride. This will help you to establish strategies to manage them effectively, so they do not hinder your leadership development.

3. Respect your superior's position of power and authority—any sign of trying to undermine their authority will stir them to resent you. As a result, they will hinder your progress. Remember, you need their recommendations to advance your career.

4. Earn the respect of your superior through your work ethic. Your superiors are interested in your production. If you prove to be faithful and innovative, they will support you.

5. Understand in depth the system you are working under. Understand the ins and outs of your organization, so that you become efficient in your work.

6. Do not fear your supervisors but respect them; they have been set apart to lead you, but they are just human. They come and go and perish like everyone else.

7. Remember, organization evolve and change. The organization that employees you today, will never stay the same forever.

CHAPTER 7

COMMUNICATIONS

THE POWER OF EFFECTIVE COMMUNICATION

In every conversation and connection, a leader must establish what and why they want to communicate. Communication is a powerful means that the leader connects with their followers.

Effective communication creates satisfaction between the audience and the deliverer. We must shift our communication from telling to connecting with each other. That means, as a leader or partner, you humble yourself to the point of experiencing what the other person world, so whatever you say will achieve its goal.

The great communicator King Solomon once said, "a person finds joy in giving an apt reply and how good is a timely word!"[130] When your communication is wholesome and healing, it rebounds back to you and gives you joy and happiness. When well-chosen words are spoken to the right person, they bring healing and life.

Effective communication gives the leader favor and grace. Healing speech that inspires people to move with purpose is the fruit of a pure heart. The grace that pours from the heart of loving leader will give them favor before great men. "One who loves a pure heart and who speaks with grace will have the king for a friend."[131] Not only will great men listen, all those who listen to them will love them and support their plans and goals. Loving talks will crown the leader with favor, and this will enable them to clarify their ideas and vision.

Effective communication provides clarity of ideas between both parties. One goal of the leader is to establish mutual understanding with their followers. If your communication is vague, it confuses your audience. If your talk is complex with difficult terms to understand, you can alienate your followers. To influence people, you must catch their hearts; you must speak at the same level with them. "The tongue of the wise adorns knowledge, but the mouth of the fool gushes folly."[132]

To speak with clarity as a leader, you must feed your brain with knowledge. To communicate effectively, you must be well-educated. "The lips of the wise spread knowledge."[133] Leaders lift the heart of the people by sharing knowledge. Leaders are the light of the followers, and knowledge is the source of light for a leader. To be an effective communicator, you must possess both knowledge and understanding.

Genuine and wise communication minimizing misunderstandings. Misunderstandings can cause conflict, loss of revenue, divorce and innocent death. Because mutual understanding connects people like magnets, it's paramount that leaders learn to communicate effectively.

Effective communication improves team building. Leaders are team builders. Leaders lead teams of people trying to create services or products to improve people's lives. The reason you learn to connect with people at a personal level is to reach mutual understanding that leads to team-building. Teams are broken because of confusion and misunderstanding between the members. A leader should facilitate an effective system that encourages open communications in their organization, family, church or country. Communication will flourish if there is trust among the members. If members are sure that the leader values their ideas and opinions, they will communicate without fear. Good teams exist to solve problems.

Effective communication helps solve difficult problems. First, to solve a problem, you must understand the root of the problem, and we must give each member of the team equal opportunity to express their view in how to solve it.

During discussion, supported by effective communication, the team will reach a mutual understanding on the problem and how to solve it. Effective communication is vital in creating flourishing organizations or families. A home that cherishes gracious talking will endure storms and come out of them safely.

Effective communication helps in communicating impactful visions and objectives of the organization. To inspire people to follow and act on your vision, you must speak persuasively, presenting your ideas with candor and power to move people to do great things. It requires energy and skill to lead a multitude to follow your ideas. A well-communicated vision changes people and inspires teams to work hard to produce great products and provide extraordinary services.

Leaders transform the lives of people and cultivate healthy behaviors. Your main goal is to alter people's experiences so they may change their behavior. Robert Greene put this way: "What changes us, and our behavior is not the actual words uttered by someone else but our own experience, something that comes not from without but from within."[134] In your communication, you are trying to create longing in people's hearts to change for the better.

Leaders do not just communicate for the sake of it, but they are moved by one desire to alter people's perception about themselves and the surrounding environment, which creates a positive mental picture that will change their minds and stir creative ideas and powerful actions that will move mountains.

Effective communication "captures people's hearts and imaginations."[135] People are not persuaded because of your fanciful words or terminology. Actions move people because you touch their hearts. You want to win people to you first, before you are asking them to follow your cause. That means, before your presentation, you may have to prepare their hearts first to receive you.

Your talk must elevate people to think great; your talk must capture people's imagination. Remember, there are no limits for human imagination. You may have to learn what your audience's aspirations are before opening your mouth.

The hearts of the wise make their mouths prudent, and their lips promote instruction. Gracious words are a honeycomb, sweet to the soul and healing to the bones.[136]

REDEFINING THE MEANING OF COMMUNICATION

Experts define communication as the art and science of transmitting messages through a medium from a sender to a receiver. When you are speaking to a friend, you are the sender and they are the receiver.

I would prefer to define communication as the visible character of a leader. The character of a leader speaks louder than words. Your character is the representation of maturity of mind, spirit and body. So, the cultivation of character is more important than your well-polished words. Out of a pure spring of water gushes words of life and healing.

Character gives you trust between you and your audience. If your character is slop, the beauty of your words won't matter. One day, your character will betray you and break trust with your audience. When I meditate on this thought, I tremble, and it humbles me, of the influence of my own habits as a leader.

What is character? Character is the product of love—the true nature of God. Love speaks through its attributes:

> *Love is patient, love is kind. It does not envy; it does not boast; it is not proud. It does not dishonor others; it is not self-seeking; it is not easily angered; it keeps no record of wrongs. Love does not delight in evil but rejoices with the truth. It always protects, always trusts, always hopes, always perseveres. Love never fails.*[137]

Who you are is the depth of your true communication with people.

As a leader, we should strive to perfect our character as we are perfecting our ability to speak. Giving powerful speeches will endure for many years, if it's supported by our good and strong character. Your words are the climax of your well-cultivated character.

THE ART OF VISUAL COMMUNICATION

Visual communication uses images, pictures or symbols that create feelings—an experience to the listeners in order to produce greater impact. Seeing is persuasive; people will judge you before you talk by how your clothes, your walk, your hairstyle, your health and the venue of your meeting. No leader should ignore the power of visually influencing the minds of their followers. Jesus led his followers a mountainside or by a lakeside to speak words of life. Your wisdom and discretion should guide you on how to cultivate your visual aids.

The impact of visual communication

Visual communication aids the audience by inducing feelings of joy or sadness. Emotions create momentum, the means of creating great services and great organization. Seeing creates a sense of presence; if I present to you with a picture of a beautiful beach in a tropical country, it creates the feeling that you are there. Moving pictures immerse our senses so much that we become part of the experience. Our brain works miracles that creates experience when we see a picture and try to find the messages that the picture is sending.

Visual communication compels your audience to take action. To encourage your audience, you must create pleasure induced by the action if they are to commit in doing the action at hand. A movie creates an urgency of actions. When we see people in action, it compels us to act. The goal of visible communication is to compel your audience to action.

They will relive the message for a long time. People remember pictures better than words. The reason behind this is that our brains work by association; if you associate numbers with pictures, it will be easier for you to remember the number. This is one reason that Jesus used parables to communicate with his audience, because they would remember the lesson for a long time. Pictures ingrain powerful emotions in our brains that are hard to forget.

You can hide a vital message in an image so that people do not comprehend the meaning of it. Sometimes it's wise and safe to hide the meaning of the message you are transmitting when there are individuals in the audience who prove harmful to your goals.

In the book of Daniel, God uses dreams to communicate with Daniel and King Nebuchadnezzar. In chapter 2 of Daniel, God gives the king a dream, and in the same manner, God reveals the meaning of the dream to Daniel. In chapter 7 of the book of Daniel, God passed to Daniel a motion picture of a great beast that represents the rise and fall of the kingdom. Dreams happen during deep sleep. "Images from a film penetrate our unconscious, communicating in a preverbal way, and become part of our dream life. Only what stirs deep within us, taking root in our minds as through and experience, has the power to change what we do in any lasting way."[138] This is the power of visual communication.

At the same time, God uses symbols and images to communicate messages to his people, like beasts, lions, bears, and leopards. Why are symbols so powerful? "Because symbols are short-cuts, they usually by-pass conscious consideration deeply, triggering embedded subconscious responses."[139]

Language is a tool created for the purpose of communicating with each other. Language has its limits; sometimes it's hard to communicate deep emotions about people and things. Deep human experiences will never be understood only with words—the best way is through symbols or an image. "Words just can't capture exactly what these experiences mean to us. We seem to pick up some deeper meaning, something symbolic that points the soul beyond the limits of human language."[140] Therefore, God uses dreams, symbols, images and visions to communicate with Daniel. Words alone cannot communicate; some messages require you to experience the world you yearn to create.

*To teach people a lesson, to real alter their behavior, you must alter their experience, aim at their emotions, **inject unforgettable images** into their minds, shake them up.*

THE ART OF NON-VERBAL COMMUNICATION

Non-verbal communication is as vital as verbal communication. Non-verbal communication is a key to unlock the potential of the communication art. "Body language is the use of physical behavior, expressions, and mannerisms to communicate nonverbally, often done instinctively rather than consciously."[141] Mediums used to pass the message can even include the place where you are presenting. For a leader to succeed in their communication, they must harmonize non-verbal and verbal communications to produce lasting impacts on their audience.

Why is non-verbal communication so powerful?

Non-verbal communication reveals our true feelings about people and things. Non-verbal communication exposes the inner thoughts that sometimes are not expressed through either spoken or written words. This means that, as the leader, you must root out thoughts that are not pure and elevating. Cultivate those ideas that will enhance the wellbeing of your followers or audience. If you feel confident about yourself, it will speak through your body. If you're authentic and secure about your own words and character, it will speak through your actions and mannerisms.

Almost 80% of communication with other people is through voice tone, gestures, clothes, facial expressions, the way we walk and the environment we are in—especially the eyes, the main door to the soul. I will not discuss the specifics of non-verbal language and their meanings; I leave this with you to explore in relation to your present culture and context.

Sometimes being skillful in observing non-verbal communication can preserve your life from evil people. People may try to hide their true motives through well-polished words, but a skillful observer will notice the true nature of their thoughts through non-verbal communication. If people are acting out of context and pushing themselves in a direction that makes you unsafe; it is wise to root out the reasons for their actions. Also, it is vital to observe your audience to know if they are paying attention to your message or if they are tired. We connect naturally through non-verbal communication.

People are unconsciously moved more by actions than words. Your actions are the greatest non-verbal language that inspires people more than your words. If your words are contrary to your actions, people will consider you a hypocrite.

A few tips to enhance your non-verbal communication

Take care of your body, mind and spirit. The spring of life starts from the fruit of your heart—your thoughts. Thoughts create emotions that propagate through your nerves and blood vessels, which cause you to behave in a certain way before your people. It's vitally important to know that the health of your physical body contributes either positively or negatively to your non-verbal communication. Feed your spirit with spiritual food and nourish your physical body with good food and exercise well. You will shine.

Hone your observation skills. Learn to specifically observe a particular expression of emotion. To behave in a controlled way is influenced greatly by knowledge of people, culture, environment and your thoughts. Study the specific meaning of various emotions as they influence people in different circumstances and environments, so you can tune yourself with them. It's vital for speakers to master how specific words provoke a specific expression in order to adapt your message accordingly.

Dress up according to the occasion. We discussed dressing properly in the section of pleasing personality. Every style transmits a specific message to your audience. If you are dressing to command respect and honor, that is what you will reap. Your followers imitate every move you make as a leader, even your style. A leader takes nothing for granted; everything is done with the objective of carrying out a goal.

Choose the venue that enhances the delivery of your message carefully. The place you choose to connect with your people has not only visual effects, but an unseen influence on your audience. The reason that non-verbal communication is so power is that it touches your subconscious mind. We are influenced by the environment without realizing it; that transforms us to follow certain behaviors without awareness. Planning the avenue to be used for public speaking should be done with care and foresight.

Be intentional about your appearance and mannerisms. Leaders are inspired by goals and visions. Nothing is done aimlessly. Learn what makes you appear attractive and decisive in your actions. Your mannerisms should match your actions in everything that you do. Visualize what you will do to stand out before your audience—this can determine your success or failure.

> My **Presence** will go with you, and I will give you rest.[142]

THE ART OF WRITTEN COMMUNICATION

The power of written words can influence millions of people with your testimony. A written word is more effective compared to any other method of communication. Technology has offered an easy means to communicate a message with the world at the speed of light. You can "tweet" and, in a second, that message is available to the entire world. Books last for many years and the reader can consult books even after the author has been dead for years.

How to make your written words effective in trans-forming the lives of many people depends on your creativity.

The art of the written word is using creative ways to make your message infectious and transformative in the lives of as many people as possible. Use written words to create an experience in the heart and mind of a listener, to alter and find a reason to adopt better habits to transform their life and those of their friends.

The power of the written word

Leaders express themselves in detail through books. It's very difficult to share all your experiences through speaking, because talking lasts for a short period. Written words are more effective because the student or audience can read at their own pace and experiment at any moment of the journey without direct connection with the author.

We can preserve written words for a long time. Think about different books that have changed the world for centuries. Historically, men have cultivated a habit of preserving written words. We have established systems that enable mankind to preserve written words for centuries. It amazes me, we still have written words on the skin of animals from hundreds of years ago.

You can consult the great minds of the world through books with ease. Learn from them many times over, with no charge! I love reading books; I can take a book with me on an airplane, into the bush, by the fire, by the lake—anywhere—and consult with great intellectuals. Dead people speak to us through books. The people who recorded their testimonies while alive keep speaking to us after they are no more. There is beauty and power in written words. Think of men such as the apostle Paul, whose letters have inspired millions of people. Leaders keep a fire burning through written words.

How to make your written words effective

Always share your experiences. Let your articles and books be your testimony. Leaders are the living word of life. They share what has transformed their lives; they are burning inward-out in blessing their followers. Inspiring books or articles are full of testimonies and experiences of leaders. I put together this book because the lessons in books changed my life and will continue to transform my life forever. Keep reinventing yourself daily, to have something new to share with your audience.

Improve your language constantly. Keep up with the evolution of language. English that was used five centuries ago is not the same as today. When people come together to form a civilization, they create language to facilitate connection. Man is not stagnant; he moves forward, never backward—so does the language. I keep learning new words and expressions to make sure that I can communicate effectively.

Language is a system of rules and principles that makes the language useful. It's vital to learn and understand the principles that govern a language. We structure many languages of the world to enhance writing. Because language is vital for the advancement of society, it must be well-organized to make sure people can communicate effectively. Leaders must learn how different principles and rules apply to the language.

Continuing to learn is a habit of great leaders. There are many styles to use in written words. Learning from great men who used the written word to influence the world will increase your usefulness as the leader. Certain styles influence a specific people. A particular style may influence scientific communities, a different in academia; your school may encourage you to use a certain style of creative writing. You may have to invent your own style to satisfy the needs of your written work. Your imagination and hard work are the limits.

> *Then the Lord said to Moses, **write** this on a scroll as something to be remembered. The Lord said to Moses, chisel out two stone tablets like the first ones, and I will **write** on them the words that were on the first tablets, which you broke.[143]*

THE ART OF VERBAL COMMUNICATION

The art of public speaking is using creative ways to connect people with a spoken word. Public speaking is the most direct way to share your experience with your followers. A leader must use their public speaking skills to influence their followers to alter habits for a better life.

The power of the spoken word

Well-chosen spoken words have divine power to heal (the opposite is also true). "From the fruit of their mouth a person's stomach is filled; with the harvest of their lips, they are satisfied. The tongue has the power of life and death, and those who love it will eat its fruit."[144] The spoken word has a spiritual power that you cannot find in written words. The spoken word has an intense power flowing through it for healing. The greatest gift that God gave to mankind is the ability to verbally communicate. A well-educated tongue will heal and create beauty in the hearts of people.

Spoken words have the living power to transform cowards into mighty warriors who go forth to conquer empires and destroy strongholds:

> The angel of the Lord came and sat down under the oak in Ophr that belonged to Joash the Abiezrite, where his son Gideon was threshing wheat in a winepress to keep it from the Midianites. When the angel of the Lord appeared to Gideon, he said, the Lord is with you, mighty warrior. Pardon me, my lord, Gideon replied, but if the Lord is with us, why has all this happened to us? Where are all his wonders that our ancestors told us about when they

said, did not the Lord bring us up out of Egypt? But
now the Lord has abandoned us and given us into
the hand of Midian. The Lord turned to him and
said, go in the strength you have and save Israel out
of Midian's hand. Am I not sending you?[145]

People are hungry to hear words of encouragement.
Leaders are generous in feeding their people with words
of encouragement and inspiration. Words give life.
Every word that proceeds from the mouth of a man
filled with the Holy Spirit will give life to the listener.
Some people are just waiting for their leader to say,
"You have what it takes to do the job." Leaders feed
your people with words of life as you feed your family
with physical food—never let them starve.

Spoken words have power to transform ignorant
people into visionary leaders. The reason that the
leader communicates through their words is to spread
knowledge and bring light to their followers. The
effectiveness of connecting with your people through
speech is that they can ask questions and have hearty
conversation that you cannot achieve through books.
Face-to-face conversation enhances natural connections that can only be achieved through mutual
presence.

Through history, leaders have used the power of the
spoken word to shape the history of the world. Here are
some key lessons I have learned through great public
speakers. Hopefully they will be a blessing to you.

Great speakers share their personal experiences and connect the large story to their followers or to the future that they are building together as a team. Barack Obama gave a speech that changed his life forever. Many believe that this speech opened the door for his presidency:

> *My parents shared not only an improbable love; they shared an abiding faith in the possibilities of this nation. They would give me an African name, Barack, or "blessed," believing that in a tolerant America your name is no barrier to success. They imagined me going to the best schools in the land, even though they weren't rich, because in a generous America you don't have to be rich to achieve your potential.*[146]

Giving a powerful speech like this is not an accident but a testimony of hard work and preparation.

Leaders spend ample time in preparation. They exhaust themselves in researching and understanding a topic before they deliver it to their followers. You cannot replace preparation with anything else. Learning how to inspire verbally will give wings to your words.

Sometimes, you may have to practice pronunciation of words to make sure that your words come out as planned. Researching the relevance of your topic will give you credibility to your audience. Working with experts in preparation will do miracles. Remember, the best speech is one which springs out of your heart.

Leaders use an impactful story to share their ideas with the audience. Most times, leaders break down their main ideas in subtopics. Here is John F. Kennedy delivering the speech "We choose to go to moon":

*We meet at a college noted for **knowledge**, in a city noted for **progress**, in a State noted for **strength**, and we stand in need of all three, for we meet in an hour of change and challenge, in a decade of hope and fear, in an age of both knowledge and ignorance. The greater our knowledge increases, the greater our ignorance unfolds.[147]*

President Kennedy connected three main points with what his audience knew and how they acknowledged themselves among others.

Powerful public leaders create a hunger, then satisfy that craving by giving a solution, such as Martin Luther King's "I have a dream" speech:

One hundred years later, the life of the Negro is still sadly crippled by the manacles of segregation and the chains of discrimination. One hundred years later, the Negro lives on a lonely island of poverty in the midst of a vast ocean of material prosperity. One hundred years later, the Negro is still languished in the corners of American society and finds himself an exile in his own land. And so, we've come here today to dramatize a shameful condition.[148]

Doctor King created a hunger in his audience by expressing the reason for their protest. As a leader, you must create a burning desire in the heart of your audience—why you want them to follow your vision.

The Spirit gives life; the flesh counts for nothing. **The words I have spoken** *to you they are full of the Spirit and life.*[149]

RECAP | EFFECTIVE COMMUNICATIONS:

1. Effective communication is the key in creating successful teams, organizations and forming healthy relationships.
2. To become a successful communicator, you must harmonize your thoughts with your values which produce powerful actions that transform lives.
3. Remember: Your body language is the use of physical behavior, expressions, and mannerisms to communicate non-verbally; often done instinctively rather than consciously. Harmonize your mannerisms with your mission to help achieve your objectives.
4. Remember: Your words have the power to give life and to destroy people. So, if you desire to transform people to a better life, change your words first, then encourage them to follow the way.
5. If you want your ideas to live for long time and to influence many people, put your thoughts and ideas on a paper. Write letters and books to inspire many others.

6. Learning and improving your communication skills never ends—always search for better strategies to connect with your people effectively.

CHAPTER 8

VISIONS AND PROPHETIC VISIONS

DEVELOPING AN INSPIRING VISION AND MISSION

For any person to streamline their path, they should avoid activities that add nothing to their growth, use their time wisely, use their energy proportionally and conduct their behavior to the high calling of their work. Developing an inspiring vision statement is crucial.

Before I explain the meaning of vision and how to develop one, we must understand the purpose and what a mission statement is.

PURPOSE

Purpose is the reason for your existence and is directly connected with your values. The values you establish while learning about personal leadership guides you in fulfilling your purpose. Purpose is in-depth insight into who you are. You may create an organization because you identified a need to be met. Let us say that there is a shortage of sugar in your community, then you create a supply chain for sugar. The service you are offering is sugar delivery. The purpose of your organization is to provide sugar to your community.

Let us look upon another example of identifying and understanding your purpose. Why were you created by your Creator? Why did He create you? What kind of need did the Lord find in His kingdom that you could fill? To answer these questions, let's go back to the beginning, during the creation of the world. In the book of Genesis, the Lord outlines the reasons he created you.

If we want to know why we are here on Earth, we must ask the Creator. The Lord said, "Let us make mankind in our image in our likeness."[150] "Image" here means we can choose, create, think and love like our Creator— we are not robots. "Likeness" means God designed us to bear His character of love. The main purpose of God creating us is to reflect His wisdom and character to this world. God extended His love by making us. The creation of man was done out of generosity from the Maker. Mankind exists to represent God and to work for Him.

The purpose of Daniel and his colleagues in working in the Babylonian court was to represent God in Babylon. They lived to represent the character of God. They did not worship the gods of the Babylonians or share in their evil practices because they understood their reason for being in Babylon.

Here is King Solomon explaining the purpose of man: "Fear God and keep his commandments, for this is the duty of all mankind."[151] We were created to manifest God's character in the world. Love God with all your heart and energy and love your neighbor as you love yourself. To live for God is the main duty of man. Your creator expressed His love for you by creating you; in return for His grace, we must express the same love to His created work. Now, how do you fulfill God's purpose in your life? By doing His work! His work is our mission.

MISSION

A mission statement expresses the work that an organization or an individual does. A mission statement answers the following questions: What is your work? Where do you work? Who are you serving or to whom is your service directed? How do you do your work? Again, understanding our mission as mankind will help us create an effective mission statement for an organization or individual.

We turn back to our Creator: "God created humankind, so they may rule over the fish in the sea and the birds in the sky, over the livestock and all the wild animals, and over all the creatures that move along the ground."[152] From the beginning, mankind was created to rule over God's created work. After God finished creating the world, He pondered, "Who will help Us take care of our created work? Who will be our manager, steward, leader to oversee Our work?" Then God said, "Let Us create a man in Our own image so they may rule and take care of creation."

God gave this world as a trust to man. God formed a home for Adam, a garden—the headquarters—and gave it to him as a gift: "The Lord God took the man and put him in the Garden of Eden to work it and take care of it."[153] The work of Adam was to take care of the garden and to rule the entire creation of God. This was the mission of Adam and his descendants. So, all mankind is to represent God's wisdom, intelligence, knowledge and character in the mission of representing Him in this world.

Daniel's mission statement developed like this: Daniel was the servant of the living God. Daniel served his God through his prophetic gift to enlighten the world about the knowledge and character of God. In the same way, Daniel worked faithfully in serving his earthly masters, the kings, in every task assigned to him, collaborating with his coworkers to ensure the success of the king's order.

Knowing your purpose and mission does not tell you where you will be in the future. You fulfill the purpose of your existence by fulfilling your mission, but what is the end goal of your hard work? Work is a blessing, but without an end goal, your hard work is useless. You work blindly without knowing whether you have reached your destination or you're working toward a wrong destination.

Take a mental picture: you're the captain of a big ship in the vast ocean, sailing without a specific destination. Yes, you are doing the right work—working hard and battling storms—but you will perish. Why? Because you will squander your resources and end up nowhere, getting destroyed by dangerous animals or exhaustion. You lacked the end goal of your hard work. Vision is a leader's end goal, the insurance of their hard work. Leaders are captains leading people to a specific destination.

VISION

What is vision? Vision is the picture we hold of how we see ourselves, sometimes five years away, ten years or forever. Vision is what we are striving to become. That means we are becoming, every day, that picture we hold in our minds. We gear all our hard work to achieve that end. We can pause and ponder: are we heading toward our destination? Or must we alter our course to align ourselves with the picture in our mind? Now our work becomes pleasurable, because we know where we are heading. We can learn from our Designer.

Here is the vision that the Lord had when creating man: "God blessed them and said to them, be fruitful and increase in number; fill the earth and subdue it. Rule over the fish in the sea and the birds in the sky and over every living creature that moves on the ground."[154]

God gave leadership to man. Since the creation of man, this has been the vision that the Lord has given to him. When God was planning to create mankind in His divine wisdom, he saw the world full of blessed people who faithfully lead in taking care of His creation. He saw a big family of loving and righteous people scattered around the world. The crowning work of God was to see mankind fill the Earth with His glory for eternity.

The Lord made all the necessary preparations for mankind to fulfill this end goal. As a leader of God's people, what is your end goal? What is your vision? Where are you taking God's people? If you answer these questions following God's example, Your Creator is proud of you. He will honor the work of your hands, and He will bless your offspring.

This might have been Daniel's vision statement: Through his work, the world will be enlightened to glimpse the character of God and His mercy, and through his prayers, Jerusalem and her people would be restored to her former glory.

This is what Daniel worked so hard to achieve in the palace of Babylon. What is your individual mission and vision statement? Having crystal clear perspective of where you are going will give pleasure and joy while you surmount stormy waters.

A few principles to remember while developing your vision statement:

1. Know your purpose (personal or corporate values) and the mission of your existence.
2. Explore your skills, strengths and weaknesses in depth. Align your mission and vision statements with your strengths, skills and talents.
3. Vision must inspire the organization or the people to be better daily, to strive for higher ground.
4. If the vision is corporate during development, you must encourage all those involved to contribute their expectations.
5. You must communicate the vision to yourself and the organization. Use all the communication techniques to inspire your people to live and strive to achieve their end goal.
6. Embody the vision. Be the vision. Breathe your vision to your people. Let everything about you be the vision or the picture you intend to achieve.

PROPHETIC VISIONS

We learned about vision and defined it as a picture that one holds that represents what they are becoming and strive to become. This kind of vision is not enough for the leaders of God's people. Besides leadership's visionary eyes, there is prophetic vision. Prophecy is an ordained divine method of foretelling future events. Prophecy gives us a vision of what future developments would look like. The main purpose of prophetic visions is to encourage and prepare the people for the future.

There are three key functions of prophetic messages. The prophecy reminds the people where they come from, the current situation and divine future events.

The role of a prophet starts by reminding the people where they come from and the reasons for their existence. For instance, Isaiah, Jeremiah and Ezekiel all reminded the people of their main purpose of existence—they existed to shed light to heathens of the mercies and glories of the true God. They encouraged the children of Israel to reconnect with the laws and regulations of God. The Lord redeemed them from the hands of Pharaoh, and He led them to the Promised Land.

These prophets reminded the people how, through different kings, God had led them through prosperous and perilous times. Daniel took the same role by praying for divine intervention for the exiled children of Israel in Babylon.

The work of a leader is the same as the prophet— to remind the people where they come from and the reason for their existence. It's easy for followers to forget their original purpose and wander aimlessly, doing what pleases them and losing the direction of their sacred mission.

The second role of the prophet is to open the minds of the people to see their current situation with clarity. In the times of the prophets Isaiah, Jeremiah and Ezekiel, the nation of Israel turned against God and corrupted themselves by worshipping idols. The children of Israel trampled on the law of God. Powerful people took advantage of the weak. The judges did not give justice and people deceived each other. The state of the nation was lawlessness. The prophets were there to remind them where their moral compass pointed, hoping that the people would seek the mercy and forgiveness of God.

For a leader of God's people, their sacred duty is to remind people of their current situation without pampering them. If they are morally strong and keep in touch with divine guidance, the leader must appreciate their efforts. If the organization is meeting its obligations and achieving its goals and objectives, the leader must reward the members.

A leader must identify opportunities and the best way to seize them for the benefit of all people. If the people need to change and improve their behavior to achieve better success for the entire team, the leader must inspire them to strive toward that end.

The last role of a prophet is to prepare people for future events as foretold by God. The prophet is the eyes and ears for a nation and her leaders. Both Isaiah and Jeremiah foretold the rise of Nebuchadnezzar as a mighty king, but they referred to him as a servant of God. They foretold that Israel would be taken captive for 70 years by Nebuchadnezzar because of their sins. After 70 years, Jerusalem would be restored to her former glory. The prophecy told the people the ordained divine events that would overtake the people of God.

This is very critical, because it helps to prepare people mentally and physically to pursue the future. Those who prepare for the future will own it. Jeremiah encouraged the people to own property, to pray for the wellbeing of the city of Babylon and to keep marrying and forming families, because they would live in Babylon for a long time.

The only way leaders can benefit from the prophetic gift is to align themselves in spirit of harmony with God's prophets. Who is the bearer of the vision for the future? The book of Daniel bears a great and valuable message for our generation. Daniel Chapter 2, 7-12 speaks a prophetic message for the time of the Babylonian empire to the end of the ages. Leaders who pay attention to these prophetic revelations will be preserved and avoid many disappointments.

Other important prophetic messages are in Matthew 24 and the book of Revelation. Jesus foretold the fall of Jerusalem, which happened in 70 AD. Those who heeded the warning of Jesus saved their lives, but those who ignored it paid with their lives.

The difficulty comes because there are so many people who claim to be prophets of God. How do you know who is a true prophet and who is not? Many leaders and governments are deceived by so-called messengers from God. Here are biblical ways of identifying a true prophet:

First, a true prophet will never contradict prophets in the Bible who proved to be servants of God. The Spirit that inspired Moses is the same that will inspire a true prophet of God today. The message of Isaiah builds on Moses, Samuel, Elijah and Elisha. The message of Jeremiah was a continuation of Isaiah's. Ezekiel was coherent with Jeremiah. The same principle applies to today's prophets. If the one who claims to be a prophet contradicts a faithful servant of God, pay keen attention to that leader because they are a deceiver.

Second, prophetic events predicted by the prophet must come to fruition per his words. If they do not happen, God did not send the man. God is not a liar; He will not give a message that will never come to fruition.

Last, the conduct of the prophets must be consistent with the character of God, which is the law of God. If the prophet does not love God with all their heart, their role is in question. If he does not love his fellow men, then they are a liar. You cannot claim to be a servant of God and deny the living power of His Word in your private life.

Our mission and vision must be married to prophetic wisdom. Prophetic vision helps us to examine if ourselves, our work and our commitment aligns with the will of God. If our work does not prepare us for the future, we have a wrong perception about the future; and we are doomed.

One of the greatest lies that have been promoted by blind leaders is that we own the future, that we are the masters of our own ships. This world belongs to the God. God is the Master of this planet, and He owns each person; He can twist the future how He wants. Aligning with His wisdom will make us prosperous and blessed with His glory.

RECAP | DEVELOP AN INSPIRING VISION AND MISSION:

1. As a leader, you must understand the purpose of your existence. Everything exists for a specific purpose. Your organization exists for a specific reason. You exist for a specific purpose.
2. To channel your energy and keep a steady momentum, you must develop an inspiring vision and mission. You may benefit greatly by learning from great leaders who accomplished wonders because they had inspiring visions and missions.
3. To prepare for the future and avoid surprises, you must pay keen attention to the word of prophecy. Prophetic visions provide guidance for the future. You must use all the principles provided by the scriptures to distinguish true and false prophets.

CHAPTER 9

THE TEST OF CHARACTER

BEFORE YOU'RE HONORED WITH POWER AND GLORY, YOU WILL BE TESTED

In your leadership service, life will test you to prove you're worthy of honor and trust. Everyone born under the sun will be tested to prove if they are worth being trusted with a blessing from God. No one can avoid spiritual tests—this divine-ordained method shapes God's people character. The test reveals flaws in character and shows if the alliance is anchored in God or this perishing world. Also, tests measure if you paid attention during your training.

Nature tests plants to show if they are worth being trusted with the blessings of nature. Windstorms shake the trees, and nature preserves those trees that are flexible and adaptable, but the wind destroys the weak and rigid ones. The trees that grow in winter must be tested to prove if they can sustain cold, and the one which fails dries up and perishes.

Animals in the wild are tested to prove if they can thrive in their ordained dominion. Animals that cannot learn to adapt to the forces of nature are swept away. Nature will test every animal accordingly, to prove if they have the skills needed to flourish in the wild.

Character will determine who will thrive and who will perish under the harsh forces of nature governed by the laws of God. A well-balanced character is the product of applying the laws of God faithfully in one's daily living. Laws do not have mercy or forgiveness; when you break them, they will break you. Both the spiritual and physical realms are governed by divine laws, and these laws are protected and administered by God Himself—anyone who breaks them will pay the penalty. Tests show if we have matured in obeying the laws of God or if we are lacking in character.

You can only develop your character through training and discipline, through trials and pain (refer to chapter 2). There is no escaping this course; every being will be tested and given a chance to develop their spiritual powers. Every time a leader dodges a test or trial, the pain that they are avoiding will double. If they keep compromising, the next trial will bring more pain compared to the previous one. If they continue to disobey the laws of God by compromising, the pain is added more and more until their fate is decided by heavenly watchers (consult Daniel chapter 4). When the seal is placed on an individual, they are bent for rebellion;

there is no returning to the path of righteousness. That individual is doomed forever.

If a leader daily resolves to obey God and His laws through thin and thick, then nature and God reward that individual with heavenly gifts. Those gifts can only be entrusted to those who are faithful, applying the living laws that God has ordained to rule over the affairs of man and nature. There is one thing I must explain before we go further: character is formed through combinations of thousands of thousands of choices that we make in life.

Character will determine your destiny. Character is paramount in the life of a leader. A leader with a weak character will make poor decisions that will bring their downfall and the destruction of their people. A leader with a strong and balanced character will make hard but necessary decisions to ensure the happiness and prosperity of their people. When we are choosing leaders, we must pay attention to their character as a deciding factor. To understand the vitality of character in the life of a leader and the tests that they will endure in their leadership tenure, we must look to Daniel chapter 6.

THE TEST OF CHARACTER – PART I
IN THE LION'S DEN

In chapter 6 of the book of Daniel, when Daniel was around eight years old, he was tested. To recap the life of Daniel, he was sent into exile by God's providence, assigned as a student of leadership in Babylon for three years and tested with unclean food.

Daniel faced annihilation with the wise men of Babylon, but through his faith in God, he was preserved. The wise men were tested to explain the dream that troubled King Nebuchadnezzar concerning his throne, and Daniel passed with glory. As if this was not enough, Daniel was tested again to explain the writing on the wall; through the leading of the Holy Spirit, he overcame the test. The heaviest test came when he was old. The test came with a threat of death and humiliation if he did not yield to the pressure. Let's discuss how the test unfolded.

Daniel is trusted with a position of power and authority by King Darius

It pleased Darius to appoint 120 satraps to rule throughout the kingdom, with three administrators over them, one of whom was Daniel. The satraps were made accountable to them so that the king might not suffer loss.[155]

Daniel's character distinguished him among all other leaders. "Now Daniel so distinguished himself among the administrators and the satraps by his **exceptional qualities** that the king planned to set him over the whole kingdom."[156] Daniel's star shone brighter than his partners' because he respected the values he set during his early days of leadership training. Even after almost 60 years, Daniel's values had not changed; purity of thought, hard work, integrity and faithfulness ruled his public service.

Daniel, in cooperation with God, worked hard and cultivated the abilities that set him above his colleagues. The superiority of his mental abilities was not an accident but involved hard work in applying the means that God had made available to His servant. If you want people and God to trust you with greater responsibility in your work, wherever you are, develop your talents to the highest standard possible. Employers and mankind are looking for men with special abilities to solve difficult problems.

Daniel's coworkers became jealous of his work ethic

At this, the administrators and the satraps tried to find grounds for charges against Daniel in his conduct of government affairs, but they could not do so. They could find no corruption in him because he was trustworthy and neither corrupt nor negligent. These men said, we will find no basis for charges against this man Daniel unless it has something to do with the law of his God.[157]

The world is looking for men who are trustworthy and faithful, like Daniel. When his accusers examined Daniel's life to find fault in his work as the government official, they could find nothing. There will always be people lazy to develop their talents and will feel jealousy against your humble heart and superiority of character. They will invent lies to destroy you.

The evil and corrupt men mislead the King:

So these administrators and satraps went as a group to the king and said: "May King Darius live forever! The royal administrators, prefects, satraps, advisers and governors have all agreed that the king should issue an edict and enforce the decree that anyone who prays to any god or human being during the next thirty days, except to you, Your Majesty, shall be thrown into the lions' den. Now, Your Majesty, issue the decree and put it in writing so it cannot be altered under the law of the Medes and Persians, which cannot be repealed." So, King Darius put the decree in writing.[158]

Selfish leaders will try to find a reason to destroy you. They will try to find if there is some misdoings on your part, so they may accuse you and destroy your reputation. If they find nothing, they will use manipulation to misguide your superiors to get rid of you. The test comes when your position of authority is threatened; more importantly, the means of earning your daily bread is put in jeopardy. This is the moment a leader must summon their internal strength to stand without wavering.

Daniel maintained his faithfulness by ascribing thanks and praise to God through prayer

Now when Daniel learned that the decree had been published, he went home to his upstairs room where the windows opened toward Jerusalem. Three times a day he got down on his knees and prayed, giving thanks to his God, just as he had done before.[159]

Daniel never crumbled under the pressure but kept his habit of praying daily. He defied the royal decree in order to worship God. You may say he could forgo prayer for 30 days and preserve his life; God would understand. Daniel understood that if he stopped praying, his connection with God would be hampered, and he would be in great danger of losing his own soul and salvation. He risked his life to honor the God of Heaven. But his accusers realized that Daniel was still faithful to his God.

The vile leaders accused Daniel before the King

They said to the king, "Daniel, who is one of the exiles from Judah, pays no attention to you, Your Majesty, or to the decree you put in writing. He still prays three times a day." When the king heard this, he was greatly distressed; he was determined

to rescue Daniel, and he made effort until sundown
to save him.[160]

Had the king known the true motives of these men influencing him to act, he would have refused to sign the law. The king tried to use all means available to save Daniel from the den of lions, with no success. The king understood who Daniel was; his character was visible to him from the beginning. Daniel's success depended on his faithfulness to the King of Heaven. The punishment was inevitable, and the only hope was that God would intervene.

Daniel is thrown into the den of lions

So the king gave the order, and they brought Daniel
and threw him into the lions' den. The king said to
Daniel, 'May your God, whom you serve contin-
ually, rescue you!'[161]

Daniel was ready to die because of his faithfulness. The king now realized that he had put in danger an innocent man who was worth more than all the other foolish leaders; he hoped that God, who had led Daniel for 80 years, would intervene for His servant. The king devoted the whole night in prayer for Daniel. Now, the king had to learn the same lesson of faith and submission to earn protection from the King of Heaven.

The Lord protected Daniel
from the hungry lions

Daniel answered, 'May the king live forever! My God sent his angel, and he shut the mouths of the lions. They have not hurt me because I was found innocent in his sight. Nor have I ever done any wrong before you, Your Majesty.'[162]

Daniel won! He was an overcomer; Daniel triumphed over death. Daniel overcame over the power of hungry lions. Heaven sent watchers to protect the faithful servant of God. God could have killed the evil administrators before they carried out their scheme, but God allowed them to succeed in point of arrogance. When man's protection cannot go farther, God will protect. What is impossible with man is possible with God. The ill intentions of our accusers work glory to the faithful servant of God; the spirit of evil men will turn against the possessor.

The accusers take the place of
Daniel in the den of lions

At the king's command, the men who had falsely accused Daniel were brought in and thrown into the lions' den, along with their wives and children. And before they reached the floor of the den, the lions overpowered them and crushed all their bones.[163]

The poison that you intend to give others, you will drink yourself. The trap that the enemy places on the path of the faithful will trap themselves. Every harm that is directed to the faithful servant of the living God will overtake the originator. Your enemies will be destroyed by your God. Never focus on them; focus on your God. When Daniel was accused by his colleagues, he never accused them back. We should learn to trust God—forgive our enemies and let God work on our behalf. Our duty is to keep doing the work assigned to us by God.

Through resolve, Daniel maintained his integrity; the God of Heaven is honored among the heathens

"I issue a decree that in every part of my kingdom people must fear and reverence the God of Daniel. For he is the living God, and he endures forever; his kingdom will not be destroyed, his dominion will never end. He rescues, and he saves; he performs signs and wonders in the heavens and on the earth. He has rescued Daniel from the power of the lions." So, Daniel prospered during the reign of Darius and the reign of Cyrus the Persian.[164]

God crowned His servant with glory and honor. The entire kingdom knew who Daniel was, knew who his God was, and his accusers vanished, leaving Daniel with more freedom to influence the world for his God. Those who overcome the test will be crowned with precious riches of this world, and after, the crown of glory in the kingdom of God. Daniel continued to prosper into old age.

THE TEST OF CHARACTER – PART II
THE BURNING FURNACE

In the previous section, we learned about the test that Daniel had to go through, but God delivered him out of it with mighty hands. Daniel was tested hard. In this section, his colleagues are tested even before Daniel was put in the lions' den. There is a saying, "Show me your friends and I will tell you what kind of person you are." As you will see, developing close friendships with people who have the same values as you are vital in advancing your career as a leader: it's worth emulating.

King Nebuchadnezzar made an image of gold, big and tall, set it up in the plain of Dura in the province of Babylon and summoned all his officials from the provinces to attend the dedication of his god. He gave a command: "As soon as you hear the sound of the horn, flute, zither, lyre, harp, pipe, and all kinds of music, you must fall down and worship the image of gold, whoever does not fall down and worship will immediately be thrown into a blazing furnace."[165]

After they sounded the music, all the people bowed down to the image, but some astrologers came before the king and accused three Jews: Shadrach, Meshach and Abednego, who did not worship the idol, and the king became exceedingly furious. The king gave them another chance to bow down to the image, when they heard the music. Shadrach, Meshach and Abednego replied to him:

> *King Nebuchadnezzar, we do not need to defend ourselves before you in this matter. If we are thrown into the blazing furnace, the God we serve is able to deliver us from it, and he will deliver us from Your Majesty's hand. But even if he does not, we want you to know, Your Majesty, that we will not serve your gods or worship the image of gold you have set up.*[166]

So, the King ordered the furnace to be heated seven times, and commanded the soldiers to chain Shadrach, Meshach and Abednego to throw them into the fire. The fire was so fierce that the soldiers died from the heat waves.

After throwing these young men into the fire:

> *King Nebuchadnezzar leaped to his feet in amazement and asked his advisers, "Weren't there three men that we tied up and threw into the fire?" They replied, "Certainly, Your Majesty." He said, "Look! I see four men walking around in the fire, unbound and unharmed, and the fourth looks like a son of the gods." Nebuchadnezzar then approached the opening of the blazing furnace and shouted,*

"Shadrach, Meshach and Abednego, servants of the Highest God, come out! Come here!"[167]

These Hebrew men came out of the furnace, unharmed, with not even a smell of smoke on their clothes. From there, the king ordered his entire kingdom to bow down to the King of Heaven. Anyone who disobeyed the command should "be cut into pieces and their houses be turned into piles of rubble, for no other god can save in this way."[168] Shadrach, Meshach and Abednego were promoted in the province of Babylon.

Key leadership lessons to reflect on:

Creation of an image or an idol for the purpose of worshiping: An image or idol is anything that takes the place of God in Heaven. Anything that distracts your attention from the true Creator. Examples include food, clothes, wealth, sex and self-exaltation. Leaders will be tested to create false gods, to turn from the true source of life, wisdom, power and glory. Success can be another god to some leaders. Creation of gods will lead to worship of the idol you created.

Worship is the service of giving praise and adoration to the King of Heaven. Only God deserves our worship. Worship is a spiritual act that places God first in your life. If you love money more than God, that is worship. If you love work more than God, that is worship. If you cherish the sin of indulgence in your life more than self-sacrifice in services to your friends and God, that is worship. Worship results from our recognition of who God is. Worship requires time. To overcome the sin of false worship demands the power of the will to ascribe your praise and honor to the Creator of the universe.

Resolution to obey God at all cost: These men made up their minds to follow God's command at the cost of their lives. Resolution is a conscious decision to follow certain principles, values or doctrines, despite difficulties or even loss of life. Resolution requires a combination of intelligence, courage, determination and self-sacrifice.

These men were clear in their answer to the king, that they would never dishonor the God of Heaven, no matter what. There are values in your life you should never compromise, despite the outcomes. For example, when the word of truth has been presented to you and the Lord has made His precepts clear to you.

Remember, even if we die because we trusted our Heavenly Father, He will resurrect us like Jesus. Leaders do not forget that Jesus died; his Father did not prevent His death, but he raised him victorious as the mighty King of Kings. Death is not final—it is a fulfillment of all righteousness. You should never sell your soul to the devil, no matter the storm he throws on you. Keep trusting.

Soldiers heated the furnace seven times: The Hebrews followed the Lord with firmness. The trial was increased, perhaps to frighten them into changing their resolution, but they followed their God into death.

Every time you resolve to follow the Lord, the devil will increase the trials to deter you from committing to the Lord.

The moment you resolve to conduct morning or evening worship in your house, problems will increase: a baby crying, sickness, tiredness, an increase of activities. All these are to discourage you from following the Lord. When these times come, patience and perseverance is the key.

The presence of the Son of God amid the fire: The king threw three men into the furnace, but in the fire's midst, he saw four men. Who was the fourth one? He was Jesus. Amid trials, Jesus is present; in pain, Jesus is present. He will send his angels to take care of you when you're in trouble. I do not know if these young men knew that Christ was amidst them. But the onlookers saw the fourth person. It's unnecessary that you see Jesus walking with you; faith will assure you of his presence. The righteous shall live by faith, never wondering if the Lord is leading them; follow His words and you have all the assurance of His abiding power and protection.

Shadrack, Meshach and Abednego came out unharmed but strengthened in God's power to save: They would have never known if God could save from the furnace of fire had they not been thrown into it. Trouble will come in this life that will cause you to doubt if you will come out the other end safe. Trust in the Lord, and you will come out victorious. Leaders are called by God and their followers to overcome adversity. I can assure you; storms will come your way—you cannot hide, you cannot escape—the only path to victory is facing them head on, with faith in God's promises. Every test that you pass opens another door to greater service.

They got promoted in the province of Babylon: When you overcome a test or trial, God will honor you, both with temporal blessings and eternal treasure. Keep trusting in the Lord. Jesus overcame the devil and death; God made him the crowned King of His dominion, of all visible and invisible things.

King Nebuchadnezzar honored God throughout the Babylonian empire: When a faithful servant of God overcomes trials, the name of God is glorified by both angels and men. We learned that the purpose of God for mankind is to represent His character on Earth; by doing so, the entire world is enlightened to His glory. We are deposits of God's character in this world. A crown of glory awaits those who overcome. Overcomers are those who put their trust in God and His son Jesus and keep working for their Master's glory and honor.

RECAP | BEFORE YOU'RE HONORED WITH GLORY AND POWER, YOU WILL BE TESTED:

1. Every leader will be tested in some point in his leadership development. The purpose of being tested is to prepare you for more usefulness.

2. Your values system will be tested to show if your house is built on a solid rock or on sand, because it is a sure thing that a storm will strike your house in a day you least expect.

3. Great leaders who shaped the world in a powerful way, were willing to lose everything even unto death to stand firm for their values.

4. The Leaders who overcome adversity are honored by God, nature and people.

5. God is faithful and able to protect his people in any danger that befalls them. Even if God does not choose to save them from death and pain, they still maintain their alliance to God, knowing that God is able to raise them from the dead.

6. God is honored among unbelievers, when his people stand firm in faith to his promises, despite dangers and hardships.

CHAPTER 10

LEAVING A LASTING LEGACY

THE ULTIMATE GOAL OF AN INFLUENTIAL LEADER

There are events in human life that you cannot avoid, such as death, changes of season and aging. A leader must live with this reality in mind, and they should match their ambition and hard work with these elements of life; if they do not, life will surprise them.

A leader must know that death will come in life; it may be today, tomorrow or ten years from now. Death should humble all of us. When we realize we are just flesh that decays and turns to dust, it behooves us to conduct our affairs with discipline and humility at heart. As a leader of a corporation or a family, if death strikes you today, what are you leaving behind? Have you prepared leaders who will take the reins and ensure the survival of your entity? Have you established a well-cultivated character that your followers will follow with passion? Have you created a sustainable system that will grant security to those you leave behind? These are some questions a leader must answer as they prepare.

Changes of season happen to us all. A leader may have to resign, maybe because of health issues, the end of their tenure, or it is the best for the organization to have a fresh mind. Whatever has happened that you must let go of power, are you prepared? Whether you created a company, or you have been selected by your followers to lead them, the time will come that you must let go of power. Here is the wisdom of a visionary leader. They prepare themselves for if this day should come. They create conditions that ensure the continuation of their leadership.

Leaders will inevitable grow old. Old age comes with wisdom but also with its challenges: loss of strength, disease, loss of momentum to push through life's storms. A wise leader will prepare for these events. There are some positions that, until death do you part, you still hold authority, like being a parent. Leaders prepare themselves for these rainy days.

All these elements of life are sign posts for a leader to cultivate their legacy. Powerful leaders live in the minds of people forever. We still remember Abraham, though he died almost 4,000 years ago. We are still learning the beautiful character of Moses, though he died over 3,000 years ago. Daniel, the man who we have been learning from, lived over 2,500 years ago. Leaders are in the business of preparing their legacy. Your legacy as the leader of the people will ensure a flow of life to the next generations. The prosperity of future generations depends on what you do today.

THE MEANING OF LEGACY

Legacy is the way people should remember you after you have passed on or after passing your leadership role to the incumbent leader. At the end of everything, your legacy will be a record of your intentional living and how you impacted the world for the better. Your legacy will determine your destiny forever. Your character is your legacy.

The Christian perspective on leaving a legacy will raise your standards even higher—to the golden gates of eternity. The discussion in the following sections gives you an example of how you should prepare your legacy.

ADAM'S LEGACY

The creation of man was the crowning work of God's character. God created Adam to be the bearer of His own character. God passed the seed of His beautiful character to Adam so that Adam may pass it to his offspring. The Everlasting God, moved by His own love, created man. The growth of Adam both spiritually, intellectually and physically, as he followed the footsteps of his Creator, delighted his Maker. It was the duty of Adam to nurture the seed that God had planted in his heart. The seed, which is the character of God, was to be developed from glory to glory and passed to his offspring.

But Adam disobeyed his Maker by eating the fruit that his Creator forbade him to touch. God took the beautiful robe of righteousness from Adam and his wife, but God never took away the seed of his character in Adam. Though sin marred the world, God never left Adam without hope or a plan of redemption. The Lord promised Adam the coming Savior; now it was the work of Adam to prepare a generation that would be ready to receive the Savior. This became Adam's consuming desire.

The Lord blessed Adam with two sons: Abel and Cain. Adam taught them the character of God and the strict obedience of His law. He taught them the plan of salvation and their duty to carry on preparing for the coming Messiah. They were to seek forgiveness through shedding the blood of innocent lambs as the symbol of redemption that the Savior would bring to mankind.

As Adam was observing his sons to see who was faithful and ready to carry on his legacy after his death, he saw the love of God in Abel. But Cain killed his brother Abel. Adam saw that the hope of his desires crushed and, seeing the character of deceit and murder flourishing in his son Cain, it crushed his spirit. The hope of passing his character to the next generation was doomed. The only way was to turn to the Creator for another son.

The Holy Scripture testifies: "Now Adam had a son in his own likeness and image."[169] As Adam observed the physical, intellectual and spiritual development of his son Seth, he saw the light in the tunnel. Adam threw himself wholeheartedly into cultivating the character of Seth, who became the father of the righteous generation where the Messiah would be born. Through the line of Seth, we have Noah, the bearer of the righteousness of God.

NOAH'S LEGACY

But as man increased in the face of earth, evil, prevailed in every corner of the earth. Man became a devouring fire. The evilness of mankind reached the throne of God. God fetched out in all the earth to see if there is a righteous man who will carry on the character of God. The Lord, the Supreme God, decree to destroy all life on the earth because of evil. Every thought of man was evil, they accepted shedding of blood of innocent which was abomination on the sight of God. Then Noah found favor in the eye of God: Noah was a righteous man, blameless among the people of his time, and he walked faithfully with God.[170]

The righteousness of God was found in this man. The beautiful character of God was produced in this man.

The Almighty God commanded Noah to build an ark; selected animals and himself and his family would be preserved during the Flood. The Lord destroyed mankind and started afresh with Noah. After the

Flood was over, Noah came out of the ark, and the Lord again passed His blessing to Noah: "Then God blessed Noah and his sons, saying to them, Be fruitful and an increase in number and fill the earth"[171] Noah became the father of all mankind on Earth. To ensure the survival of the next generation, the Lord made a covenant with Noah:

And God said, "This is the sign of the covenant I am making between me and you and every living creature with you, a covenant for all generations to come: I have set my rainbow in the clouds, and it will be the sign of the covenant between me and the earth. Whenever I bring clouds over the earth and the rainbow appears in the clouds, I will remember my covenant between me and you and all living creatures of every kind. Never again will the waters become a flood to destroy all life. Whenever the rainbow appears in the clouds, I will see it and remember the everlasting covenant between God and all living creatures of every kind on the earth." So, God said to Noah, "This is the sign of the covenant I have established between me and all life on the earth."[172]

After Noah did his work faithfully, he preserved the line of righteous people. God entrusted the work of preparing a nation that would represent the kingdom of God on Earth to Abraham.

ABRAHAM'S LEGACY

Abraham found favor in the sight of the living God because he believed in God. God made a promise to Abraham that, through him, all nations would be blessed. This is the testimony of God concerning Abraham: "Abraham will surely become a great and powerful nation, and all nations on earth will be blessed through him. For I have chosen him, so that he will direct his children and his household after him to keep the way of the Lord by doing what is right and just, so that the Lord will bring about for Abraham what he has promised him."[173]

Abraham was recommended because of his willingness to prepare a people who would represent God. When you study the life of Abraham, you realize that he did everything he could to prepare for the coming of the Messiah and for the nation of Israel to be a blessing to the world.

God assured Abraham because of his faithfulness:

"I swear by myself," declares the Lord, "that because you have done this and have not withheld your son, your only son, I will surely bless you and make your descendants as numerous as the stars in the sky and as the sand on the seashore. Your descendants will take possession of the cities of their enemies, and through your offspring all nations on earth will be blessed, because you have obeyed me."[174]

The prosperity of the next generation depends on their founding father. The Israelites were blessed because of Abraham's faithfulness. I wonder, will God bless the next generation because of you?

Manifesting the character of God on Earth was passed to Isaac by Abraham, who passed to Jacob, and Jacob passed to his son Joseph, and Joseph passed to the descendants of Israel. The nation of Israel under their leaders were depositories of the mercy and grace of the living God to the world. Through Juda's offspring, the Messiah was born, the King of Kings.

JESUS'S LEGACY

The birth of Jesus marked the fulfillment of the promise that God made to Abraham. Jesus is the image of the invisible God manifest in the form of man. Christ lived among men and lived a pure life that represented the character of God. Jesus represented his Father on Earth; Jesus made the character of God clear through his conduct among men. Jesus restored God's righteousness that was lost in Eden through his death on the cross. The sacrifice of Jesus gave access to the throne of God for every believer.

Those who believe in Jesus have forgiveness of sin and the righteousness of God in them. Through Christ, we have everlasting life, because he died and was resurrected from the dead. The fullness of God has been made complete in us through Christ Jesus. After Christ finished his work on Earth, He passed his legacy to his

disciples before he ascended to his Father. Here are
Christ's words to his followers:

> *When he had finished washing their feet, he put
> on his clothes and returned to his place. "Do you
> understand what I have done for you?" he asked
> them. "You call me Teacher and Lord, and rightly
> so, for that is what I am. Now that I, your Lord
> and Teacher, have washed your feet, you also should
> wash one another's feet. I have set you an example
> that you should do as I have done for you. Very truly
> I tell you, no servant is greater than his master,
> nor is a messenger greater than the one who sent
> him. Now that you know these things, you will be
> blessed if you do them."[175]*

Jesus commands his followers to do the same as He
has done. This is the command to every generation,
to live like Jesus lived among men, to represent the
character of God as He did. We must also carry on
the promise of resurrection, as Abraham taught and
believed in the Savior's coming. We must teach the
world that Christ is coming again, and those who
believe in Him have everlasting life.

This hope, the everlasting living legacy of the Savior,
is to be reproduced in our lives. The world must behold
the robe of righteousness of God on us, as one beholds
the rising of the sun. We are the bearer of God's glory
in our character. The testimony of Jesus, as the first
born from the dead, must propel us to witness to others

of this living hope. We are not living for now but for
eternity.

EVERLASTING LIFE

Elijah and Elisha raise people from the dead through
the Living Name of the Everlasting God. They did not
raise people from the dead through their own power,
but as the testimony of the One who was to come from
above.

Jesus offered himself to be the light of the world
and, through His breath, every living creature receives
their being. Christ testifies that he is the resurrection
and revealed himself as the giver of life in resurrecting
Lazarus from the dead. Through the power of the Holy
Spirit, Jesus knew that Lazarus was dead, and this what
he said to his disciples:

> "Our friend Lazarus has fallen asleep; but I am
> going there to wake him up." His disciples replied,
> "Lord, if he sleeps, he will get better." Jesus had been
> speaking of his death, but his disciples thought he
> meant natural sleep. So, then he told them plainly,
> "Lazarus is dead, and for your sake I am glad I was
> not there, so that you may believe. But let us go to
> him."[176]

When they arrived at the tomb of Lazarus, Jesus
commanded the people to take away the stone, and he
called Lazarus to come out. Lazarus came out a living
being. This was to show his followers that the Father

had given Jesus the power to raise the dead. The way Jesus called Lazarus from the dead is the same way he will call those sleeping in Christ to wake up and meet their King.

Leaders are the bearer of the Good News to the world. Those who live with faith in Jesus will rise up again; the death that we experience is temporary rest for believers. We carry this legacy that the Lord has left for us. Everything that we do reminds us we will die someday, but God will raise us from the dead. Our work of leading does not end after death; we will resume it after we unite with the King in his second coming. The character that we develop now in partnering with Heaven will determine our destiny.

Jesus showed us the Father; he revealed His character to mankind, and he showed us how to live a life of honor and service in representing our Heavenly Father:

> For I have come down from heaven not to do my will but to do the will of him who sent me. And this is the will of him who sent me, that I shall lose none of all those he has given me but raise them up at the last day. For my Father's will is that everyone who looks to the Son and believes in him shall have eternal life, and I will raise them up at the last day.[177]

Christ was here to do the will of the Father, and the will of the Father is that everyone who believes in the Son has everlasting life. Christ represented the Father, lifting mankind to believe and obey the Word from God. After he finished his work, he proclaimed before the Father, "I have finished the work You in trusted in me." The Father was honored through the legacy of His Son. Now the Savior has given us the same task, to represent him before all mankind so that whoever believes in Jesus will have everlasting life.

Every human being will recount the trust given to him by God. The Lord will raise all the people to recount their lives. Jesus will resurrect the righteous to everlasting life and the evil to eternal destruction.

GIVING AN ACCOUNT OF YOUR DEEDS

We learned that God trusted the leadership of Earth to mankind. We are the stewards of God's creations; because we do not own God's creation, the owner will require an account of our leadership. Leaders, we will give a report of our work. More important now, we are the stewards of the grace of God manifested through the life, death and resurrection of Jesus Christ.

Not only that, we will be accountable for the great commission trusted to us by Jesus, as the bearer of the gospel of salvation to the world. This is the legacy that Christ left for us to follow. This is the legacy we must pass on to our children. Abraham did his work, and he passed the legacy to his offspring; they finished the work of restoring the kingdom of God. Jesus did his work, the apostles did their work, the reformers finished their task, and now the torch has been passed to us.

All mankind, from Adam to the last born of the world, will stand before the Living God and the holy angels and give account for every deed. This is how serious this meeting will be, because everyone will have to give account on the day of judgment for every empty word they have spoken. "For by your words you will be acquitted, and by your words I will condemn you."[178] We learned that words give life, and through words, we can kill and destroy. Leaders inspire through words. Words reveal the treasure of the heart.

Angels record every word that comes out of the mouth of a leader in the books of Heaven. Either they produce life or death—they will condemn you or be your testimony of a well-lived life. If we give an account of our words and deeds, how much of our inner thoughts, which were never revealed to others?

The Son of God who bought us with his precious blood says, "Look, I am coming soon! My reward is with me, and I will give to each person according to what they have done."[179] The King of Kings, the Supreme Leader of all the holy angels and the universe says, "Be ready, I'm coming soon to reward everyone according to their works."

The leadership of your own body, your family, all those around you, was given to you by God. He will demand an account of your time, energy, money, life, mind and talents. Take a moment of reflection on how you spend your time; will you be able to stand as a faithful steward? Leaders, we must redeem time. Let us work for the Master, so that when He comes, He finds us working and blessing the world.

Daniel, the man who we have learned leadership from his life, had the heavens opened to him in a vision of the day of judgment. These are his words:

> As I looked, thrones were set in place, and the Ancient of Days took his seat. His clothing was as white as snow; the hair of his head was white like wool. His throne was flaming with fire, and its wheels were all ablaze. A river of fire was flowing, coming out from before him. Thousands upon thousands attended him; ten thousand times ten thousand stood before him. The court was seated, and the books were opened.[180]

This will be an open hearing for everyone. The fallen angels, with their arch deceiver, will also give an account of their lives. Evil deeds will be revealed for everyone to see. When the court sits, that means there is punishment as well.

If a leader was lazy and unfaithful to his Master, they will be condemned for eternity. My friends, the Lord and His people may trust you with power, authority and glory; you may abuse your power and oppress your fellow people. You will give an account of your actions; you will receive proportional to your deeds. The greater your responsibilities are, the greater your accountability will be before God. Leaders, desire and aspire to hold a powerful position but remember to conduct yourselves honorably, because you will give an account according to your responsibilities.

Solomon—the wisest leader who ever lived; the man crowned with wisdom, knowledge, insight, power and authority; the man who was loved by God; the man who the entire world loved and desired to sit at his feet to listen and absorb his wisdom; the man who built mansions and a powerful kingdom rival to none; the man who made gold walking stones in Jerusalem—became proud and arrogant and turned his back against the oracles of God.

He followed the pleasures of this life as far as he could go—married 1,000 wives, assembled the most accomplished musicians he could find and searched for every possible way of enjoying life—but at the end, he recanted his life and committed himself to preaching and educating leaders through proverbs, songs, parables, poetry and wise sayings. This is how he counseled the leaders-in-making:

> *Now all has been heard; here is the conclusion of the matter: Fear God and keep his commandments, for this is the duty of all mankind. For God will bring every deed into judgment, including every hidden thing. whether it is good or evil.*[181]

RECAP | LEAVING A LASTING LEGACY:

1. All great leaders understand that they are the testimony of those leaders who came before them.

2. One of the main tasks of a leader is to prepare leaders who will carry on their mission, when they are no more.

3. Leaders keep in their mind the big picture of what they are trying to achieve which will become their legacy.

4. Leaders remind themselves that they are accountable to their people and God. One day they will give an account of their works.

5. Christian leaders are entrusted to carry on the legacy that Jesus left for us: To prepare a people to receive the kingdom of God; To remind people that they are here to develop character for eternity; To encourage people to keep believing that they have assurance of resurrection from the dead through Christ Jesus.

6. Leadership does not end here, being a leader will continue for eternity. Whatever we do here prepare us for the future usefulness in the kingdom of God.

ENDNOTES

Preface

1 White, Ellen G. *"Prophets and Kings (1917)."* Copyright 2017. Ellen G. White Estate, Inc., n.d., 884. Pg. 485

Chapter 1

Leadership | An overview of leadership

2 Blanchard, Ken and Renee Broadwell. *Servant Leadership in Action: How You Can Achieve Great Relationships and Results.* Oakland, CA: Berret-Koehler Publishers, Inc, 2018. Pg. 39

3 Ibid. Pg.8

4 Proverbs 29:18 (KJV)

5 Maxwell, John. Leadershift: *The 11 Essential Changes Every Leader Must Embrace.* USA: Harper Collins Publishers, 2019.) Pg. 23

6 Von Clausewitz, Carl. *On War.* Penguin Group, 1832.

7 Ecclesiastes 2:14

Chapter 2

Training Ground | An opportunity to learn how to become an effective leader

8   Daniel 1:3

9   White, Ellen G. "*Patriarchs and Prophets (1890)*." Copyright 2018 Ellen G. White Estate, Inc., n.d., 707. Pg. 216

10 Genesis 37:28

11 Matthew 4:1-2

12 Galatians 1:15-18

13 Genesis 12: 4-5

14 Genesis 15:2-5 (KJV)

15 Genesis 26:1-3

16 Genesis 28: 5

17 Deuteronomy 8:2-5

18 Deuteronomy 8:2-5

19 White, Ellen G. "*Prophets and Kings (1917)*." Copyright 2017 Ellen G. White Estate, Inc., n.d., 884. Estate, Inc., n.d., 884. Pg. 49

20 "*Understanding Intuition and How the Mind Works.*" Psychology Today. http://www.psychologytoday.com/blog/in-one-lifespan/201209/understanding-intuition-and-how-the-mind-works

21 Ecclesiastes 7:19

22 Ecclesiastes 9:14-16

23 2 Corinthians 12: 9

Chapter 3

Student of Leadership | The qualities of a student of leadership

24 Daniel 1:3

25 Proverbs 18:21

26 John 6:63

27 Proverbs 18:20

28 Amen, Daniel G. *Change Your Brain, Change Your Life: The Breakthrough Program for Conquering Anxiety, Depression, Obsessiveness, Lack of Focus, Anger, and Memory Problems.* New York, NY: Harmony Books, 1998. Pg. 156

29 Genesis 15

30 Genesis 28:10-22

31 Genesis 37

32 White, Ellen G. *"Christ's Object Lessons (1900)."* n.d., 278. Pg 212

33 Greene, Robert. *Mastery.* (New York, NK: Penguin Group, 2012). Pg 26

34 Ibid. Pg 30

35 Graham, Stedman. *Identity Leadership: To Lead Others You Must Lead Yourself.* New York, NY: Center Street, 2019. Pg. 107

36 Greene, Robert. *Mastery.* New York, NY: Penguin Group, 2012. Pg. 27

37 Graham, Stedman. *Identity Leadership: To Lead Others You Must Lead Yourself.* New York, NY: Center Street, 2019. Pg. 107

38 *"A Quote by Abraham Lincoln".* https://www.goodreads.com/quotes/140440-all-i-have-learned-i-learned-from-books. Accessed October 4, 2019.

39 1 Samuel 10:23-24

40 1 Samuel 16:18

41 *"John F. Kennedy Quotes."* BrainyQuote. https://www.brainyquote.com/quotes/john_f_kennedy_130752. Accessed September 10, 2019.

42 Martin, Karen. *Clarity First: How Smart Leaders and Organizations Achieve Outstanding Performance.* New York: McGraw-Hill Education, 2018. Pg. 237

43 The Oracles. *"10 High-Achieving Execs Share the One Quirky Trick That Turned Their Dreams into a Reality."* Business Insider. https://www.businessinsider.com/how-10-top-executives-made-their-dreams-into-a-reality-2019-8. Accessed August 19, 2019.

44 1 Kings 12:4

45 1 Kings 12:7

46   1 Kings 12:10

47   1 Kings 12:16

48   *"Top 10 Greatest Speeches."* Time. http://content.time.
      com/time/specials/packages/article/0,28804,184122
      8_1841749_1841745,00.html. Accessed September 11,
      2019.

Chapter 4

Personal Leadership | The starting point for greatness.

49   Drucker, Peter F. *"Managing Oneself."* Harvard Business
      Review. January 1, 2005. https://hbr.org/2005/01/
      managing-oneself.

50   Daniel 1:8

51   White, Ellen G. *"Prophets and Kings (1917)."* Copyright
      2017. Ellen G. White Estate, Inc., n.d., 884. Pg. 485

52   Daniel 1:11-15

53   Covey, Stephen R. *The 7 Habits of Highly Effective
      People.* https://theedge.solutions/wp-content/
      uploads/2018/08/Covey-The-7-habits-of-highly-
      effective-people.pdf. Accessed November 10, 2019. Pg.
      41

54   *"For CEOs, Integrity Is the Best Policy."* Yale Insights.
      May 24, 2019. https://insights.som.yale.edu/insights/
      for-ceos-integrity-is-the-best-policy.

55   Daniel 6:10

56   Daniel 2:17-19

57   Daniel 9:3 (KJV)

58   Proverbs 12:26

59   Proverbs 12:26

60   Proverbs 22:24-25

61   Proverbs 27:17

62   Proverbs 13:20

63   Ecclesiastes 4:9-12

64   Peale, Norman Vincent. *The Power of Positive Thinking*. The Quality Book Club. Ebook version copyright 2006, n.d., 286.

65   Daniel 7:16

66   Daniel 7:19-20

67   Daniel 9:1-3

68   Daniel 9: 21-23

69   Proverbs 27:23-27

70   White, Ellen G. *"Thoughts from the Mount of Blessing (1896)."* n.d.,116. Pg. 64

71   Daniel 4:9

72   Daniel 5:10

73   Daniel 5:10-15

74   Daniel 6:3

75   Acts 4:32

76   Wetterlin, Cory. *"Ellen G. White's Understanding of Indwelling of the Holy Spirit: A Chronological Study."* Andrews University Seminary Student Journal: Vol, 1: No. 2, Article 5. 2015. https://digitalcommons.andrews.edu/aussj/vol1/iss2/5. Pg. 19.

77   Daniel 1:17

78   Daniel 1:9

79   Daniel 6:3

80   Daniel 2:46

81   Daniel 2:48-49

82   Daniel 5:29

83   Daniel 1:9

84   Daniel 10:8

85   Daniel 10:12

86   White, Ellen G. *"Prophets and Kings (1917)."* Copyright 2017. Ellen G. White Estate, Inc., n.d., 884. Pg. 484

Chapter 5

Problems | Solving difficult and complex problems

87   Martin, Karen. *Clarity First: How Smart Leaders and Organizations Achieve Outstanding Performance.* New York: McGraw-Hill Education, 2018. Pg. 44

88   Daniel 2:15

89   Daniel 2:16

90   Daniel 2:17

91   Daniel 2:18

92   Hebrew 11:1, 6

93   Daniel 2:19

94   Daniel 2:20-23

95   Daniel 2:24

96   Daniel 2:25

97   Daniel 2:27

98   Acts 12:20-23

99   Daniel 2:47-48

100 Daniel 2:49

101 Daniel 4:4-18

102 Daniel 4:9

103 Daniel 4:9

104 Daniel 4:20-23

105 Daniel 4:24-26

106 Daniel 4:27

107 Daniel 5:10-16

108 Daniel 5:17

109 Daniel 5:18-24

110 Daniel 5:26-28

111 Daniel 5:29-30

Chapter 6

Superiors | Dealing with personnel of power and Authority

112 Daniel 4:27

113 Daniel 1:11-17

114 Abrashoff, Captain D. Michael. *It's Your Ship: Management Techniques from the Best Damn Ship in The Navy.* New York, Boston: Grand Central Publishing, 2012.

115 Daniel 6:21

116 Daniel 5:18

117 Daniel 4:19

118 Daniel 6:4-5

119 Abrashoff, Captain D. Michael. *It's Your Ship: Management Techniques from the Best Damn Ship in The Navy.* New York, Boston: Grand Central Publishing, 2012.

120 Daniel 4:32

121 Genesis 4:6-7

122 Genesis 4:8

123 Genesis 4:9

124 Genesis 4:9

125 Genesis 4:10-12

126 Genesis 4:13

127 Daniel 2:30

128 Daniel 2:27

129 Ecclesiastes 3:1-8

Chapter 7

Communications | The power of effective communication

130 Proverbs 15:23

131 Proverbs 22:11

132 Proverbs 15:2

133 Proverbs 15:7

134 Greene, Robert and Joost Elffers. *The 33 Strategies of War.* New York: Penguin Group, 2007. Pg. 401

135 Hennessy, John L. *Leading Matters: Lessons from My Journey.* Stanford, CA: Stanford University Press, 2018. Pg. 131

136 Proverbs 16:23-24

137 Corinthians 13:4-8

138 Greene, Robert. and Joost Elffers. *The 33 Strategies of War.* New York: Penguin Group, 2007. Pg. 402

139 https://thoughtsdrawnout.com.au/symbols-are-short-cuts-for-our-brains/

140 https://www.psychologytoday.com/us/blog/light-and-shadow/201305/more-words-five-ways-unleash-the-power-synbols

141 Greene, Robert and Joost Elffers. *The 33 Strategies of War.* New York: Penguin Group, 2007. Pg. 396

142 Exodus 33:14

143 Exodus 17:14, 34:1

144 Proverbs 18:20-22

145 Judges 6:11-13

146 *"Barack Obama's Keynote Address at the 2004 Democratic National Convention."* 2004. PBS News Hour. July 27, 2004. https://www.pbs.org/newshour/show/barack-obamas-keynote-address-at-the-2004-democratic-national-convention.

147 *"John F. Kennedy Moon Speech."* n.d. https://er.jsc.nasa.gov/seh/ricetalk.htm. Accessed June 22, 2019.

148 King, Martin Luther. *"I Have a Dream."* American Rhetoric. n.d. https://www.americanrhetoric.com/speeches/mlkihaveadream.htm. Accessed June 15, 2019.

149 John 6:63

Chapter 8

Visions and Prophetic Visions | Developing an inspiring vision and mission.

150 Genesis 1:25

151 Ecclesiastes 12:13

152 Genesis 1:26

153 Genesis 2:15

154 Genesis 1:15

Chapter 9

The Test of Character | Before you're honored with power and glory, you will be tested

155 Genesis 1:15

156 Daniel 6:3

157 Daniel 6:4

158 Daniel 6:6-9

159 Daniel 6:10

160 Daniel 6:13

161 Daniel 6:16

162 Daniel 6:21

163 Daniel 6:24

164 Daniel 6:26-28

165 Daniel 3:5-6

166 Daniel 3:17-18

167 Daniel 3:19-26

168 Daniel 3:29

Chapter 10

Leaving a Lasting Legacy | The ultimate goal of an influential leader.

To order more copies of this book, find books by other
Canadian authors, or make inquiries about publishing
your own book, contact PageMaster at:

PageMaster Publication Services Inc.
11340-120 Street, Edmonton, AB T5G 0W5
books@pagemaster.ca
780-425-9303

catalogue and e-commerce store
PageMasterPublishing.ca/Shop

ABOUT THE AUTHOR

Erick Shogholo studies great leaders who have shaped the cause of humankind — influential leaders in business, science, military, politics, social fields and religions as well as great leaders recorded in the Bible. He also, employs his mind in observing, interviewing, learning and experimenting with the best leadership principles that will improve the effectiveness of leaders in their homes, business, government, churches, relationships, and in managing difficult problems.

He was born in Tanzania, Kilimanjaro Region and moved to Canada in 2008. He graduated with a Business Administration degree from Burman University and founded InsightLeaders Group Inc.

InsightLeaders Group creates and designs solutions to empower people to apply proven leadership principles. The WisdomApp is available for iOS users to help empower your leadership journey. Erick also teaches Biblical based leadership principles through the InsightLeaders YouTube channel.

Erick's mission is to help people improve their lives through the application of rock-solid leadership principles. He helps leaders connect with their fellow leaders, and with God, allowing them to draw strength and wisdom, resulting in improved effectiveness in leading their followers and impacting their communities.

www.ingramcontent.com/pod-product-compliance
Lightning Source LLC
LaVergne TN
LVHW051456080426

835509LV00017B/1782